A Bloomsbury Canvas

A Bloomsbury Canvas

Reflections on the Bloomsbury Group

Edited by Tony Bradshaw

With essays by

James Beechey • Anne Olivier Bell • Julian Bell • Quentin Bell
Tony Bradshaw • Angelica Garnett • Henrietta Garnett • Craufurd Goodwin
Jane Hill • Hermione Lee • Virginia Nicholson • Nigel Nicolson
Frances Partridge • S.P. Rosenbaum • Richard Shone • Frances Spalding

Lund Humphries

First published in 2001 by

Lund Humphries
Gower House
Croft Road
Aldershot
Hampshire GU11 3HR

and

131 Main Street
Burlington
VT 05401-5800
USA

Lund Humphries is part of Ashgate Publishing

British Library Cataloguing in Publication Data
A catalogue entry record for this book is available from the British
Library

1003402994

Library of Congress Control Number: 2001093177
ISBN 0 85331 839 5

Designed and typeset in Goudy Old Style
and Garamond ITC Narrow
by Mark Bradshaw, Sherborne, Dorset
Produced for the publishers by
John Taylor Book Ventures
Faringdon, Oxfordshire
Printed in Italy by EBS, Verona

TITLE PAGE
Vanessa Bell
Calendar Design (1930s)

For all the good friends who have graced

The Bloomsbury Workshop

over the years

Contents

'Of all the Bloomsbury legacies, the greatest is their concept of friendship. Nothing – not age, nor success, nor rivalry in art and love, nor separation for long periods by war, travel or careers – ever parted these people who came together when they were young.'

Nigel Nicolson

Duncan Grant
Barns and Pond at Charleston (1934)
A watercolour study for *A Sussex Farm*; the pond and barns remained favourite subjects for the Bloomsbury artists.

Vanessa Bell
Decorative Design with Urn (c.1933)

Introduction

Tony Bradshaw

The telephone rang. 'Is that The Bloomsbury Workshop?' I acknowledged that it was. 'Well,' said the voice at the other end, 'I wonder if I could order some wood?'

Despite the possible connotations with the woodworking industry, in one mind at least, The Bloomsbury Workshop, tucked away in a little courtyard near the British Museum, is in fact a gallery and bookshop specialising in the art and literature of the Bloomsbury Group. Started by myself in a very modest way in 1986 as a part-time diversion from the exigencies of the City and a full-time indulgence in an all-consuming hobby, the Workshop has welcomed through its doors over the years a diversity of academics, collectors, curators, art historians, bibliophiles and other assorted enthusiasts from around the world – all bound by the common passion for Bloomsbury. Not only have the visiting enthusiasts enjoyed the changing fare of paintings, drawings and books, scarce or new, but the endless communications from as far afield as Alaska, Namibia, Israel and Tasmania have been further testimony to Bloomsbury's international appeal.

So what explains this far-flung fascination? And what exactly is 'Bloomsbury'?

There are, of course, no easy answers to these questions, questions that have absorbed historians for decades. A small coterie of writers and artists (and one economist) working in England in the first half of the twentieth century, the circle came on its name by accident, as a joke among friends. Certainly within their own lifetimes the central members of Bloomsbury were dismissive of any notion of a cult or clique, and Clive Bell came to be so resentful of sniping attacks on the ill-defined 'Bloomsbury' that he even tried to suggest at one point that a Group had never existed. However, there is no doubt that a grouping of some nature did exist, if only as a loose association of friends. The fact that a peripheral member, Molly MacCarthy, forged the word 'Bloomsberries' and E.M. Forster in 1929 was to state authoratively that Bloomsbury was 'the only genuine movement in English civilisation' must lend credence to the notion that the participants themselves were fully cognisant of its importance, and their place within it.

At its simplest, the Bloomsbury Group was the circle round Virginia Woolf and Vanessa Bell. When the Victorian man of letters Sir Leslie Stephen died in 1904, his daughters, Virginia and Vanessa, being determined to put their constrained middle-class girlhoods behind them, set up house at 46 Gordon Square in the then-shabby district of Bloomsbury with their two brothers, Thoby and Adrian. Thoby brought home his Cambridge friends Leonard Woolf, Clive Bell, Lytton Strachey and Saxon Sydney-Turner, inviting them for social evenings with his sisters, the scene being set of earnest youths sitting around the room sipping cocoa and whisky and discussing intently such matters as the 'meaning of truth'. Most of these young men had been elected to the Apostles, a secret society of intellectually notable undergraduates from Trinity and King's Colleges. Through the link with the Apostles the Group widened to include E.M. Forster, Roger Fry, Desmond MacCarthy and John Maynard Keynes who had left Cambridge earlier. The Group also included Duncan Grant, Lytton Strachey's cousin.

Apart from Saxon Sydney-Turner, who remained an obscure Treasury official, all of the Bloomsbury Group made a very significant contribution to British intellectual and artistic life in the first part of the twentieth century. The two giants, famed internationally, are

Virginia Woolf, who broke new ground with her 'stream of consciousness' writing; and the economist, Maynard Keynes, whose revolutionary economic theories and significant efforts to build new economic orders after the traumas of two world wars remain an abiding legacy.

However there is no denying that in the last thirty years, since the seemingly endless flow of biographies, memoirs, published letters and diaries began, the Bloomsberries have been chiefly famous for their less than conventional personal relationships. By today's standards they may not have had a dazzling number of encounters – Frances Partridge has claimed that there was more love and less sex than people tend to assume – but the homosexuality or bisexuality or generous open-mindedness of many members of the Group permitted a fascinating web of affairs and liaisons. These ranged from the devoted partnership of Lydia Lopokova and Maynard Keynes (who had once been almost exclusively homosexual), to the open marriage at Charleston of Clive and Vanessa Bell, to the ménage at Ham Spray where Lytton Strachey loved Ralph Partridge, who married Dora Carrington, who loved only Lytton (and who took her life after his death to prove it). With Virginia Woolf committing suicide herself, the early deaths of Thoby Stephen through typhoid and of Vanessa's son Julian, killed in the Spanish Civil War, the Bloomsbury story is laced with serious drama as well as less consequential intrigues.

The fascination with the Group's lives, their work and their art has grown exponentially over the past thirty years, and The Bloomsbury Workshop, providing a focal point for the books and pictures, has significantly contributed to this increasing awareness. To complement and add interest to the varied round of exhibitions, a number of people have written short essays, a selection of which have been brought together in this book. Including the leading scholars and art historians in the field, the writers of these essays have all been intimately involved as commentators on Bloomsbury over the past quarter century. Among their number, Angelica Garnett, Quentin Bell and Frances Partridge speak from first-hand experience, as they themselves were directly involved through family ties or close association from the 1920s onwards, while both Nigel Nicolson and Anne Olivier Bell knew well a number of the main participants. Collectively these writers bring unique insights and perspectives to new corners of the Bloomsbury canvas.

The most endearing aspect of these brief essays and memoirs is that they have the air of confidences. Often far from scholarly, sometimes sketchy and always relaxed, they presume a certain level of familiarity with the Bloomsbury legend. None of the writers troubles, for example, to explain who Virginia and Vanessa's parents were or that Charleston is set among the fields of Sussex. They refer to Duncan or Lytton or Roger with the easy assumption that everyone knows the natures of these people and exactly where they fit into the story; Leonard and Clive and the others are treated, in the same way as the readers regard them, as friends or people with whom they are closely associated. That easy familiarity, almost a continuation of the original Group's relationship, is part of the mix of current-day fascination with Bloomsbury.

Another attractive aspect of these pieces is that the writers totally abandon the embattled stance and aggrieved tone that defenders of Bloomsbury can sometimes adopt. The authors know that they are among friends and yet, as if they had been asked a stimulating question over lunch or tea, they use the occasion of each essay to provide a short focal point for reminiscences, allowing for specificity and vividness of detail. Although Angelica Garnett has described her friend and second cousin Janie Bussy in her memoir, *Deceived With Kindness*, she takes the opportunity of an exhibition essay to recall Janie with greater precision, seen in memory sitting on a deckchair on the lawn at Charleston: 'Her back is cradled by the canvas of the chair, while her long elegant legs in high-heeled sandals are crossed in an unconscious gesture of self-protection and a book half falls from narrow fastidious hands. In a gauche way she was, I think, sexy, but her sensuality, detectable in the droop of her scarlet lips, remained unsatisfied.' Elsewhere Julian Bell, writing on the occasion of a small memorial exhibition of Quentin Bell's work, evocatively recalls his childhood memories of his father's absences in the adjoining pottery: 'In that other room he would be moulding or scraping or painting the clay, sucking at a pipe that had usually gone out, listening to Radio Three; happy, you felt. You knew that that quiet, steady, pleasurable activity was at the centre of him; and now it's what isn't there.'

Threaded through the essays are reproductions of paintings and drawings, all of which have passed through the hands of The Bloomsbury Workshop at some stage; selection of these has been narrowed further by the decision to exclude images published previously in any other book. While adoption of this criterion has resulted in the omission of such notable paintings as Vanessa Bell's *E.M. Forster* and *Mrs Grant*, both now in the USA, and Carrington's *Annie Stiles* and *Beeny Dogs*, purchased respectively by an Australian collector and the Johannesburg Art Gallery, the positive outcome is that a number of important and delightful images are for the first time being unveiled to a wider audience.

These pictures illustrate much of what is best and typical in Bloomsbury art. They range widely and include portraits of the artists' friends and relations; reinterpretation of noted European iconography; scenes around Charleston and from the artists' travels abroad; creations of sheer fantasy; self-appraisal, to be seen in Vanessa Bell's introspective *Self Portrait*; caricature as witnessed in her Paris café drawings; some cheerful, uplifting decoration; and an absorption (particularly by Vanessa) with flowers and vases in still-life compositions. Mixed with a dash of the exotic (*Bacchus*) and a glimpse of the erotic (Grant's supple male nudes), these images represent the very essence of Bloomsbury art that their devotees find so alluring.

What these pictures share with the essays is a sense of charm, intimacy and inspiration. And as long as people enjoy the exploration of new corners and get warm pleasure from the old stories retold, then there is no doubt that Bloomsbury enthusiasts from Southampton to San Francisco will be joined by new adherents from Rio to Reykjavik. That, after all, is what *A Bloomsbury Canvas* is about.

Duncan Grant
Abstract (c.1915)
This is a collage incorporating fabric. The same material was made into a dress by Vanessa Bell, in which she was painted by both Grant and Fry.

Plums of Memory

Angelica Garnett

Vanessa Bell
Angelica Painting (c.1932)
One of many paintings of
the artist's daughter
(b.1918).

W hen I think of London in the 1920s, with its high shadowy ceilings and Victorian basements, its linoleum-covered stairs and infinite stretches of York paving stones running beside iron railings, it spells gloom and the implied and, for me alien, demand for good behaviour. There were dancing classes in Hampstead, piano lessons in St John's Wood or tea parties at the Raverats', to which I walked or went on the bus with Louie, my nurse, dressed in coat, hat, scarf and gloves, with shoes polished and socks tightly drawn up. The effort to look the same was great but the result, I knew, was inferior to that of the other little girls encountered on such occasions. Delight in the spontaneous sensuality of life was inhibited by the conformity inherent it seemed in the bricks and mortar, the busy roads and eternal noise of London.

The appeal was, and more or less had to be, to the mind rather than to the senses, and mine was sluggish, resisting Rose Paul's effort to teach me arithmetic and spelling in her neat, shining but somehow alien schoolroom in Mecklenburgh Square. I shone, frailly, only when required to recite poetry or draw from life a highly treasured pottery eagle that stood on her mantelpiece. These moments of self-fulfilment were crowned with cosy success when the three mothers, Mrs Nelson, Gwen Raverat and Vanessa, refreshed and supported by cups of tea, sat on the small sofa under the window, listening to their three daughters' performance of such poems as 'I remember, I remember, the house where I was born …' which epitomised for me my nostalgic craving for Charleston.

When it was at length time to go there, it was the arrival and not the journey that mattered, knowing as we did that it was a beginning to long weeks of summer holidays – day after day of pleasurable, even ecstatic sensations untrammelled, or almost, by the oughts and shoulds

OPPOSITE
Vanessa Bell
Iris and Narcissi (c.1950)
A scene in the garden
room, Charleston. The
painting incorporates a
decorative roundel by
Duncan Grant.

of convention. Louie fought her own battle for behaviour, but under the umbrella protection of the grown ups I could often afford to disregard it. Feet went bare, hair unbrushed and my skimpy frocks were as often as not stained with paint or blackberry juice. The garden contained our intimacy and sometimes our clashes of opinion, while outside stretched the sleepiest of Sussex cornfields, hemmed in only by the noble curve of Firle Beacon. In those days the passionate cooing of the wood-pigeons or the plaintive mooing of cows were the most insistent among the noises off.

All this, it seemed, was not only controlled but had been created by Vanessa in the same spirit attributed to God when He created the world. She had stretched out her hand and lo, Charleston, the Downs, the Weald and the watermeadows, even to a certain extent Lewes and Rodmell, Leonard and Virginia, came into existence full and complete and, during my childhood, unchanging. When, eventually, changes did occur, they were felt as a derogatory, underhand chipping away at a vision that had, in its day, however old fashioned or inconvenient, been near perfect. Vanessa, from her place at the dining-room table, carving the joint or pouring out coffee, was demonstrably our only necessity. Life without her was inconceivable and when she did, very occasionally, absent herself, I immediately developed mumps or cut my finger on a new penknife, or some unexpected guest arrived who, with the best will in the world, turned everything topsy-turvy.

Vanessa Bell
Wallflowers (c.1915)

Vanessa had another, equally significant place however and that was at her easel, from where her gaze, although benign, was nevertheless concentrated in all its abstract remoteness on ravishing combinations of colour, light and shade with which she seemed to carry on a constant communion. Separated from but aware of the habitual noises and rhythms of life in the background, she never lost touch with the Ariadne-like thread which connected her careful hand and large grey eyes to the subject. Neither did she forget the demands of family life. When some inner sense of time, or the coolness of the evening forced itself on her consciousness, she would scrape her palette, tie her dirty brushes in a rag and take her box and canvas indoors, sighing with a mixture of pleasure and frustration.

It was time for pure joy to come to an end, but she was never idle. This was my hour, longed for and, I'm happy to say, appreciated, not only by me but occasionally even by Clive and Duncan, when the latter stopped painting after it was too dark to see. The garden-room fire was lit and Vanessa read aloud from the Brontës, George Eliot or, more universally appreciated, from Jane Austen. Her voice was low, cool and controlled, lending a certain dignity even to the monologues of Miss Bates or the inanities of Mrs Bennett, coming into its own with the quiet if intolerable authority of Mr Knightly and able mysteriously to suggest the final passionate concern of Mr Darcy for the distressed Elizabeth. Her greatest triumph was perhaps when I burst into tears on the death of George Osborne on the field of Waterloo … that was not at Charleston but, of all places, in a hotel not far from the Cobb at Lyme Regis. I was jealous of my friend Eve, Mrs Younger's daughter who had read *Persuasion* when I had not, and could therefore talk as an adult to Vanessa on a subject from which I was utterly excluded. But in truth Vanessa was not so much a dramatic as a tireless reader, soothing and almost hypnotic to listen to and whose voice connects me as surely to the nineteenth century as though I had lived in it myself.

Duncan Grant
Kneeling Woman (1930s)

Dora Carrington

Frances Partridge

'What was Dora Carrington *really* like?' is one of the questions that I'm most often asked about the past – and also the most difficult to answer. My usual reply is, 'Read her published letters – you'll find she has drawn her own portrait in them'; for, gifted painter though she was, she also had a wonderful way with words, and her lively, spontaneous correspondence, with its marvellously amusing and inventive pen-and-ink illustrations, will, I believe, gain her a permanent place among English letter-writers. Why should it be so hard to describe her, I wonder? Because of her originality, the quality of uniqueness she possessed, her free creative imagination that leapt over barriers and conventions to express itself; because of the life-style she had invented, her poignantly felt personal relationships, and the poetry she sensed in nature and inanimate things. Those who knew her well have tried to convey the impression she made on them – Ottoline Morrell's 'moorland pony' is one of the best; Aldous Huxley noticed the 'little gasps' in her talk and the expression of puzzled earnestness in her large blue eyes. David Garnett describes her 'bell of thick straight hair the colour of weathered straw'. To Julia Strachey she was 'a modern witch', and 'there wasn't a lover, a servant or a cat that didn't pride him or herself on being the most favoured of the lot'. Personally I would add that she kept something of a little girl about her, in the way she moved, and stood with toes turned in; in her soft cajoling voice and infectious, wholehearted laughter; in her fantastic and teasing sense of humour.

David Garnett sets first her long relationship with Lytton Strachey, and certainly it was remarkable – a deeply moving devotion to someone unable to respond to her sexually, yet whose death left her life so empty that she killed herself. In her early days with Lytton at Tidmarsh Mill he was probably dominant; his calf-bound books covered the walls, his fondness for rice pudding (endemic to all Stracheys) controlled the menus, and when he read

19

Duncan Grant
Lytton Strachey (c.1922)
Although dated 1911 by
Grant, this drawing is in fact
likely to have been executed in the early 1920s, at the
time when Strachey was
receiving great acclaim for
his biography *Queen
Victoria*.

aloud from poets and dramatists in the evenings she was very much the pupil and he the master. She cared for him tenderly when he was ill; she adored his wit. He could 'do no wrong' in her eyes. However it is important to remember that – quite apart from her professional brilliance as a painter – there was a touch of genius in Carrington's own personality and taste, something that was vividly revealed in the hospitable life of Tidmarsh and Ham Spray House, whose walls she decorated like a bower-bird. At the Slade she had been an outstanding and popular figure, setter of fashions and winner of several prizes. The painters of the past who meant most to her were Piero della Francesca, Goya and Renoir, while among her contemporaries she was strongly influenced by Mark Gertler, with whom she had her first love affair. She went on to develop the confident and striking style of *The Mill House, Tidmarsh* and the portrait of Lytton [of 1916], after painting which she wrote more seriously than usual to her sitter, 'I wonder what you will think of it when you see it. Tonight it looks wonderfully good and I am happy. But I dread showing it. I should like to go on always painting you and never showing you what I paint. It's marvellous having it all to oneself … I would love to explore your mind behind your finely skinned forehead. What a peace to be with you and how happy I was today.'

This passage is interesting in several respects. It shows her ambivalence between confidence and modesty. It reveals the secretiveness which was a marked feature of her character, and also touches on the mystery of her reluctance to show her work, particularly in exhibitions, or (except when very young) to sign it. Was this perhaps partly the result of getting no encouragement from a strict and philistine mother whom she heartily disliked? (It was her father who backed her desire to paint and she always loved him for it.) And, deeply involved as she was in her art, there may be some clue to be found in the fact that already at the age of thirty she was beginning to withdraw from serious painting in favour of charming fringe activities such as making glass-pictures and tiles. One explanation is that the 'moorland pony' passionately loved her freedom and independence; no one but Lytton was allowed to curb her. The same was true of her personal relations. She resented the desire of her admirers to 'tame' her; it wasn't that she enjoyed making them unhappy – she was not in the least cruel, but, like Yeats's mistress she 'bid them take love easy as the leaves grow on the tree'.

Dora Carrington
Boats on a Beach (c.1914)

Duncan Grant: Designer and Decorator

Richard Shone

Duncan Grant
Carpet Design (1930s)

I n the 1960s, when I first knew Duncan Grant, easel-painting was still the central preoc-
cupation of his creative day. Decorative projects and commissions were fitted around the
daily absorption in still life or portrait. Just as Virginia Woolf might rest her mind from
the rigours of fiction by writing a passage of diary before lunch or dinner, so Duncan Grant
would elaborate decorative ideas in sketchbooks once he had done his duty with oil paint on
canvas. It was 'another part of one's self at work', as he said, and the ideas often flowed,
sheet after sheet. Sometimes he worked towards a specific project; at others it was an almost
unconscious freeing of the hand. So strong, I think, was his urge towards calligraphic expression that any surface would do – from the lid of a cigar box to an important letter from his
bank or the pages of the telephone directory, within easy reach of his studio armchair.

Although, at the time of which I'm writing, the days of large decorations were over (the
Venus and Adonis opera designs and the Lincoln Cathedral chapel were the last), there was
always some smaller project to hand. There were illustrations for books (such as the Folio
Society *Monkey* in Arthur Waley's translation), designs for pottery, a three-fold screen, decorations for gramophone speakers, and a variety of objects for friends down to the humblest
bookmark sent as a birthday or Christmas present. Ballpoint or pencil was used first, then
colour added by pastel, crayon or watercolour. The design was repeated several times until it
reached a satisfactory state (it rarely came out all in one go). I think he sometimes over-
embellished what had begun as (or had quickly become) something clear and pointful. When
a project needed oil paint (such as the three-fold screen), he would quite often paint a preliminary version in oil on paper, sometimes cutting it up and shuffling the components until
the final design was achieved. These versions often had a spontaneity of handling that was
submerged in the finished version. He would carry on too long, losing an initial verve for the

OPPOSITE
Duncan Grant
Tragedy (c.1950)
This is a study for a projected
side panel for a theatrical
production at the Sadlers
Wells Theatre, London.

23

Duncan Grant
Bacchus (*c*.1935)

sake, as he thought, of laborious integrity. In contrast, some of the pottery he painted, made by Quentin Bell, keeps the freshness of design of his best decorations.

From the 1920s Grant's imagery retained its Mediterranean flavour (what wonderful illustrations he might have done for Elizabeth David!). This continued to the end – the Italianate fountain on a panel at Charleston (*c*.1968) or the two lithographs of washerwomen, excavated from memories of Cassis. Sporting gods and goddesses – the men slim, light as feathers, the women lumberingly voluptuous – stayed in the repertoire, with infinite variations of enigmatic pose and gesture. But the overwhelming idiom was of flowers and leaves, fruit and shells, lop-sided urns, pedestals, looped curtains, imagery as capable of permutation as was Vanessa Bell's handful of abstract hieroglyphics.

Much of the mythological basis of Grant's figurative designs can be found in his earliest sketchbooks. Here one sees tributes to Poussin, whose drawings he adored and copied as a student. So many influences of style and content accumulated through the years, cross-fertilised and transformed. Of special importance, I think, were French Romanesque sculpture (Vézelay for example), the Ravenna mosaics, Graeco-Roman funerary portraits and aspects of Far Eastern painting. I remember photo reproductions of the first three on the studio mantelpiece at Charleston. The Byzantine influence can be seen in costume designs for *Macbeth* of 1912; although Grant knew the Ravenna mosaics from monographs, it was only in 1913 that he saw them for himself and maintained, to the end of his life, that they were the 'greatest decorations' he had ever seen.

Duncan Grant
Design for Tiles (1957)

First and foremost, Grant was a decorator rather than a utilitarian designer. He took a given situation and 'dressed it up'. I do not know how interested he was in modernist design in the 1920s, for example, though he was certainly aware of it. He was by no means insensible to the requirements and taste of his time, but by the 1930s criticism of his decorative style had begun to appear in the press. The rejection of his murals for the *Queen Mary* early in 1936, on the grounds of unsuitability for a luxury liner, seems to have spelled the end of further large-scale public commissions, except for Berwick Church, Sussex, an ambitious but more local undertaking. It should, however, be stressed that certain aspects of international design that became common currency between the wars had been anticipated by Grant and his fellow artists in 1913 at the Omega Workshops.

If we look at Grant's decorative work as a whole it emerges as a singularly original and influential contribution which has continued to be mined by younger artists and commercial designers. Perhaps those among his early admirers will be confirmed in their opinion that Grant's true gifts lay in the realm of decoration. Certainly one might say about this aspect of his work that, unlike some of his easel-painting, it retains the freshness of his personal conception – frank, mercurial, unportentous, done entirely for pleasure.

Voyages

Angelica Garnett

With my parents, Vanessa Bell and Duncan Grant, I often went on voyages, from which however we always returned. If they were journeys out and away from English life, they were recognised as temporary escapes into a wider, more cosmopolitan world where the landmarks were none the less familiar links with both past and present, not only Raphael and Piero, but Matisse and Picasso. When we put up our easels, it was often in the vicinity of a Roman column or a building by Alberti, or in a landscape recalling Corot or Cézanne; we were infused by a feeling of continuity, a sort of spiritual kinship which, to my parents at least, was a source of pleasure and inspiration.

Vanessa would have preferred to travel invisibly, or at least incognito, enclosed within the bubble of her own dreams and abstractions, but she also took it for granted – as indeed did we – that it was her business to make all practical arrangements for our journey. It was she who went to the Wayfarers' Travel Agency, booked the tickets, did all the telephoning, had the car repaired, and left instructions for forwarding letters; she in fact who, while ensuring our safe return, took responsibility for the success or failure of our adventure.

For this is what we called it although, blessedly enough, no disasters ever happened. The excitement we felt at seeing the cliffs of Dover recede while those of Calais or Dieppe grew larger, was much like that of watching the lifting of the curtain at the theatre; but it was a curtain behind which we could actually penetrate, mixing with actors who were unconscious of the footlights, but played their role to perfection. English failings, too well known and understood, were temporarily suspended to allow the renewed enjoyment of half-forgotten but newly appreciated habits and ways of living. Such things as good coffee, good food and general kindness oiled the wheels, and we counted them as luxuries. They were, more or less,

Duncan Grant
Countryside near Ravenna (1913)
Painted on a visit to Italy in April 1913 when Grant accompanied the Bells and Roger Fry.

OPPOSITE
Vanessa Bell
Turkish Scene (1911)
Painted during a visit to Turkey with Clive Bell, Roger Fry and Harry Norton, during which Vanessa Bell suffered a miscarriage and was nursed by Fry. It is among her earliest recognisably Post-Impressionist landscapes.

the only ones: although Vanessa sometimes drove her own car, by the time it was packed it was so full that space for humans was limited and uncomfortable. Hotels were chosen for their ambience rather than for comfort: in French ones the plumbing was deficient and the electricity dim, while in Italy both were deplorable and, before the Americans had won the war against parasites, there were often bed bugs and fleas to contend with. The only thing that was nearly always good was the food – prepared with more care than now. But all these things were peripheral – enjoyed if possible, laughed at or forgotten if not. The real purpose of the excursion was a state of mind, a communion with things seen, impossible to put into words, and yet, by small interjections, sighs and signs, shared. The tempo was slow and the temperature never high, but little was missed and a lot enjoyed.

Wherever we were, daily life followed much the same pattern as at home: breakfast, with as much hot coffee as could be commanded or procured, then a pause for a cigarette and the settling of accounts, and making a plan for the day. Then the disappearance of one and all to wash, collect brushes that had been carefully cleaned the evening before and left standing in the bathroom tooth-mug, together with paint boxes, canvas or board, easel and so forth. Then to the motif, usually on foot, Vanessa's appearance reminiscent of the White Queen, Duncan's a mixture of Charlie Chaplin and an apache from the purlieus of Montmartre. He would of course help her with her paraphernalia, but if he chose to go in a different direction, it was then we might expect him to return accompanied by a new friend who was helping him with his own accoutrement. He had an extraordinary ability to concentrate on his canvas, while adding delicately little dabs of paint, and carrying on an oversimplified conversation in a foreign language, with some terribly serious and shy adolescent who fancied he too might become an artist. It may have been the strangely remote look in Duncan's eye, fastened not only on the subject but on his own vision of it, that attracted people. It was the same magnetism that operates between humans and certain animals which, while superficially friendly, proves to be incorruptibly aloof.

In Italy in particular both painters drew small crowds to watch their performance. There may be those whose temperament allows them to put on an act of painting, but neither Vanessa nor Duncan were capable of this. Vanessa would avoid such a situation whenever possible, even at the sacrifice of a more exciting view of her subject: she would choose the shadowy corner under a bridge or some ledge too small to accommodate anyone but herself.

But this wasn't always possible, and there were days she would return for lunch exasperated by the antics of small urchins who hadn't been able to resist the temptation of putting their fingers into her delicious whorls of vermilion or cobalt and smearing it on their cheeks and noses. And in Rome, her totally unjustifiable faith in human nature led her to leave our passports on a nearby stone while concentrating on the cypresses in the Medici gardens – with foreseeable results which led to hours of questioning by the Fascist authorities.

Many evenings were spent writing letters about such happenings, magnifying their importance to those at home to provoke laughter, which we at our café table would vicariously imagine, thus enjoying it twice over. After supper, when the lamps were lit and the fountains playing, we would return to our iron bedsteads and lumpy mattresses to sleep soundly, and start all over again the following morning.

Vanessa Bell
Venice (1948)
After the Second World War,
Vanessa Bell's and Duncan
Grant's summer holidays
abroad were mainly spent
in Italy. Paintings and drawings from these visits record
scenes in Venice, Lucca,
Perugia and elsewhere,
while the two painters also
made a number of copies of
Italian old masters.

Roger Fry as Painter

Frances Spalding

'Things have been less quiet here recently.' So Duncan Grant wrote to Eddy Sackville-West from Charleston in August 1926. There was no doubt in his mind as to the cause. 'Roger Fry is here, better in health, and therefore a most energetic guest as to ideas, etc. One seems to work along at a greater pace when he's about. He even paints a little as well as writes and reads us part of his new book, which I must say I think will be for me enthralling.' It did not seem right that a person, semi-convalescent, should be able to teem with ideas, produce a ground-breaking book on Cézanne *and* paint. Charleston, at its most constructive, had a settled peace conducive to painting. Roger Fry, involved with the *Burlington Magazine*, with collectors, dealers, editors and intellectuals, represented a less contemplative world. Surely he could not embroil himself in this arena and also paint?

At Charleston an opinion took root and became received opinion: Roger Fry, though a great and lovable human being, had no natural facility for paint. Vanessa Bell dreaded his retrospective, held at the Cooling Galleries in February 1931. 'The show will be very trying I expect,' Vanessa told Clive Bell. 'All sorts of things one hoped never to see again are being fished out.' Much later, in the pages of the *Charleston Magazine*, Howard Hodgkin, an artist whose sensuous involvement with his medium is pre-eminent, fiercely condemned Fry as a painter who lacked physical sensibility of any kind.

I was familiar with this negative attitude to Fry's pictures when I first began researching his life and work. Yet painting was for him central; he trained as a painter and even when other activities began to eat into his time he always regarded it as absolutely necessary to his existence. At the height of his fame he would leave England for months on end in order to paint happily on the Continent. His passion for painting informed his criticism, forming the other

Roger Fry
Venice (1929)
Painted during a visit to
Venice with his sister
Margery Fry.

OPPOSITE
Roger Fry
Nina Hamnett (c.1917)
One of a number of Fry's
nude drawings of Nina
Hamnett during their affair
in 1916 – 17. In a letter to
his former lover Vanessa
Bell, Fry wrote of Nina *'Elle
est vraiment putain* but a
very nice one and one
ought to accept that as a
type of character *comme
une autre* and not be
annoyed at it or demand
what it can't give'.

Roger Fry
Studland Beach (1911)
This is one of several paint-
ings of this Dorset beach
made on Fry's visit to
Studland with his
Bloomsbury friends.

side of the same coin. At an early stage in my research I felt it necessary to see as many of his pictures as could be found. As a result I wrote not only to friends and relatives of his, but also to almost every public art gallery in the country, making appointments to see his work. 'May I come and see one of Fry's rare early paintings?' I asked a member of the Trevelyan family. 'Do come,' was the reply, 'and please *take* it away!'

What I saw in the months that followed makes any single definitive view of Roger Fry's paintings impossible. His vigorous mind never stood still and nor did his art, one style giving way to another, in his bold forays after the motif. In the 1890s and early years of the twenti-eth century he was regarded by his contemporaries as a kind of old fogey. He abhorred the dabbling with vaguely Impressionist methods because they seemed to him to result in weak design. Instead he looked back to the seventeenth century, sat at the feet of Ricketts and Shannon who were interested in reviving Old Master methods and painted Italian villas and their gardens in a classical mood. Looking at *The Pool*, it seems almost like the calm before a storm, for who would have thought that this 'pastichist of the ancients', as D.S. MacColl dubbed him, would subsequently become the leader of the avant-garde, accused by Robert Ross of mounting a plot 'to destroy the whole fabric of European painting'?

Much has been written about Post-Impressionism in England and Fry's theoretical justification of it. As a painter he experimented readily with a Post-Impressionist language, often working on a large scale. His contemporaneous interest in mosaics encouraged his use of thick dark outlines around the edge of hills, trees or clouds. What may seem a little heavy-handed was a deliberate simplification for aesthetic purposes; Fry, who had earlier edited Sir Joshua Reynolds's *Discourses*, agreed with Reynolds's belief that particularisation usually lowers the emotional pitch of a painting and that elevation of mood (or expressive vigour in Fry's language) necessitates a strong degree of abstraction and generalisation. He was one of the first to exhibit in the new style, showing fifty-two works in a one-man exhibition at the Alpine Club Gallery in January 1912.

Roger Fry
Still Life with Chocolate Cake (c.1912)
This painting was exhibited in a show of works by English painters at the Galerie Barbazanges in Paris, 1912. Fry himself coordinated the exhibition.

Roger Fry
Le Petit Port, St Tropez
(1922)
Roger Fry spent some time
in St Tropez in late summer
1922. Writing to Robert
Bridges that October, Fry
enthused 'I enjoy myself
immensely – I can't quite
tell why – but I believe it's
nothing but the climate and
the charm of this absurd
little town'.

This is not the place to trace all the changes and developments in his art. He poured a great deal of energy into the Omega, yet never lost an opportunity to paint. One of his most successful exhibitions was that of flower pictures held at the Carfax Gallery in 1917. Nearly all sold, and Sickert praised them as 'serious and thoughtful work, full of feeling for the possible dignity of this branch of still-life, and showing appreciation of colour, growth and pictorial structure, expressed without the tedium of over-literal representation'. Once the war ended Fry left London for an extensive period in France. It deepened his love of Provence, where he was eventually to buy a simple farmhouse which he shared with Charles and Marie Mauron. It is to be hoped that one day someone will write a book about Roger Fry and France, his admiration for its various landscapes, for the light and colours of the Midi, for peasant life and customs, its more democratic attitude to culture, its architecture and artistic heritage. We can sense his pleasure at being in France in the lithographs which show him haunting the interiors of churches, farmyards and landscape, all of which are drawn with a pure love of the subject.

Roger Fry
Head of a Model (1913)
This model was painted by
Vanessa Bell on the same
occasion.

In both his lithographs and paintings we find evidence of his knowledge of art. He drew and painted with intimate familiarity with the work of Claude, Corot, Poussin and many others. His art always displays an intelligent grasp of form and composition, and a depth of feeling that owes much to his cultivated experience. When towards the end of his life he once again revised his aesthetic theories, and admitted to Helen Anrep that he was getting shockingly 'literary' owing to her influence, he looked again at the Impressionists, not his English contemporaries but the French originals, with great pleasure. The impresario of Post-Impressionism ended his painting career in a style closer to Monet than Matisse.

There is so much to enjoy in Roger Fry's paintings that it would be a pity if received opinion deprived us of the opportunity to reassess the pictorial output of one of the most fertile minds of this century. It was above all a mind familiar with the language of paint and its long history. At a time when so much art is predicated on ignorance of the past, the paintings of Roger Fry grow in stature and significance.

Remembering Quentin

Julian Bell

W hen someone dies, it can be that you miss not only their presence but the way they had of being absent. In the family home my father Quentin was away, for much of the time, in the pottery. In that other room he would be moulding or scraping or painting the clay, sucking at a pipe that had usually gone out, listening to Radio Three; happy, you felt. You knew that that quiet, steady, pleasurable activity was at the centre of him; and now it's what isn't there.

What is left is this profusion of pleasurable, often strange, often beautiful objects. These are made with an affable unconcern for canons of good taste or artistic ambition, for Quentin seemed to undertake his work in a spirit of private curiosity and absorption. And yet he was, as is obvious, fascinated by what has passed in history for good taste and for canonical beauty, and much of his imagery is a kind of wry meditation on these themes.

Quentin reflected on a large, public scale, but what he produced was generally intimate, intended for domestic use and enjoyment. Working in the long shadow of two acclaimed painters, his mother and Duncan Grant, he concentrated on the applied art of pottery, rather than on addressing the art scene they had made their mark in. This was an option for pleasure – a relish for the moist, heavy, soft resistance of the clay – and also for a kind of intellectual innocence. In the figurines Quentin's imagination often worked upon recondite stimuli, taking them through convoluted reversals; and yet it's difficult to take the sometimes bizarre results as evidence of the state of his soul when he, a thoroughgoing materialist, didn't credit the existence of any such entity. He let the character of his work emerge unselfconsciously, exploratively. It is good to think that his work, wherever it goes now, communicates some of that innocent joy.

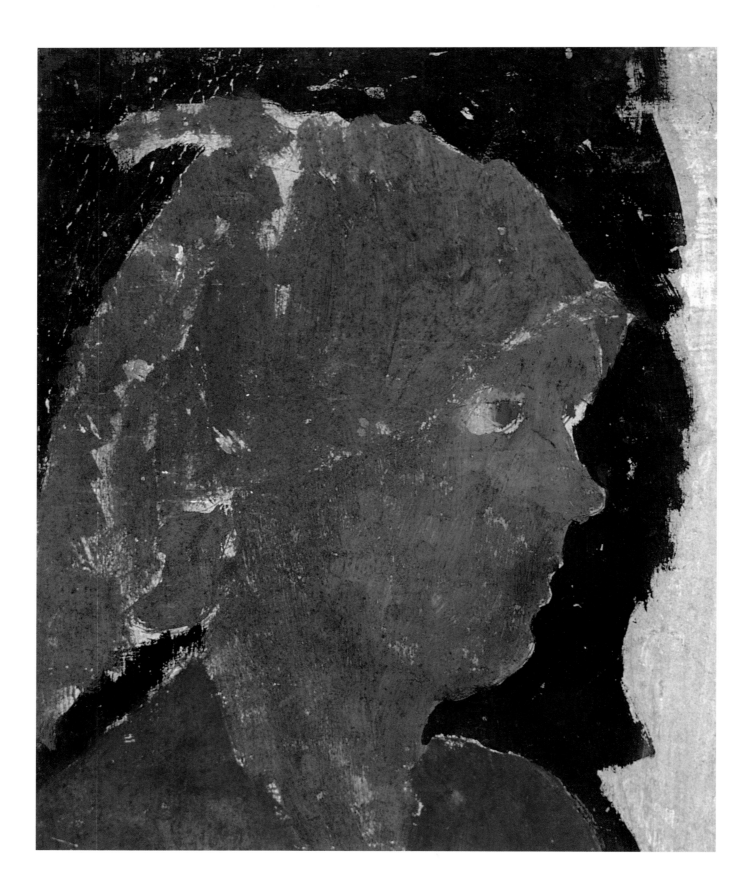

Vanessa Bell: A Personal Impression

Frances Partridge

I first met Vanessa when I was twenty-one, just down from Cambridge, eager for experience but short of confidence. She must have been about twice my age; some people found her alarming, but I'm glad to say I never did. I admired her from the first, and when I got to know her better I grew to love her. One never thought of age in relation to her, though I think she was unusually mature in her forties. Her face still possessed the noble beauty of the photographs of her as a girl, but further modelled and with its lines engraved by human emotions and response to other people. I remember with pleasure the little bunches of lines which appeared at the corners of her eyes when she was amused – which was often, her sudden outbursts of laughter, and her curved smile reminding one of a Greek statue of the Archaic period. Her speaking voice was deep and melodious – a real contralto. By the time she was fifty her thick straight hair was mostly grey. I never remember a time when her movements were not deliberate, and I doubt if she enjoyed activity for its own sake. Did she ever run? She must have, because she was a devoted mother and grandmother, and small children have to be chased at times, but in the picture called up by memory she is walking with head slightly bent (and bound with a scarf) or standing, or sitting with her hands in her lap if they aren't busy sewing, drawing or writing. Her handwriting was very much a painter's – she *drew* the letters.

It's difficult to avoid comparing her with Virginia – both sisters so brilliant, but Vanessa lovable and intensely human where Virginia dazzled and impressed.

It was at Charleston that I saw Vanessa most often before the Second World War. The way of life there was as much her personal creation as any of her paintings – an effortlessly sympathetic ambience in which she and Duncan were free to work, Clive to read and write, and all

Vanessa Bell
The Pond, Charleston
(c.1919)
In a letter of October 1916 to Roger Fry, Vanessa Bell wrote 'the pond is most beautiful, with a willow on one side and a stone and flint wall edging it all around the garden part, and a little lawn sloping down to it, with formal bushes on it'.

OPPOSITE
Duncan Grant
Vanessa Bell (c.1913)
Probably painted at Brandon, a summer camp in East Anglia where members of Bloomsbury joined several of the Neo-Pagans (the group centered around Rupert Brooke).

visitors to follow their own bents. I don't know how much hand Vanessa had in the excellent meals with an English country flavour, but I'm sure she saw that the coffee was first rate and everything was served in dishes and cups that pleased the eye. Meals were sociable times of unscripted talk and laughter; in summer chairs would be pulled out into the garden for more talk, chess or strolling among the flowerbeds, where Vanessa would collect fruit and flowers for her still lifes, but I never remember her going for a country walk.

The war cut across the meetings of friends, but after it was over members of the Memoir Club were glad to have a chance to congregate in its Bloomsbury rallying-points, generally in Vanessa's or Leonard's rooms. Vanessa was at her most lively and relaxed on these occasions, displaying her own individual comic style of talk, sometimes spiced with mixed metaphors and malapropisms. The reading of papers led to a discussion, often the best part of a very jolly evening. There were wine and biscuits, and sometimes serious problems might be considered. I remember Vanessa delighting everyone by her firm and simple verdict on one of these – it was crime and punishment. In her deepest voice she said: 'I see *no* point in punishment myself'. Equally characteristic was her reply to Duncan when he complained that some letters he wanted to read to us 'seemed to be written in invisible ink'. Vanessa: 'A pity *all* letters aren't written in that, in my opinion.'

I have described Vanessa as a hostess. It was difficult to winkle her and Duncan out of Charleston as guests; but I do remember that we once took advantage of their hot water freezing up to persuade them to spend a weekend at Ham Spray. Having got them, we were quite worried how to entertain them, but I noted afterwards that they were 'the nicest company and best guests we had had for ages, and could and did talk about anything with unfailing interest and gaiety'. Vanessa was in her mid-seventies and physically an old lady. Mentally and spiritually she seemed ageless.

Duncan Grant
*Vanessa Bell Painting at
Charleston* (1918)
This watercolour is one of a number of studies Grant executed for his painting *Interior* now in the Ulster Museum, Belfast. It shows Bell painting from the window-seat of the dining room at Charleston.

The Hogarth Press

Tony Bradshaw

'It's such a gamble,' Virginia Woolf wrote of the Hogarth Press to her sister Vanessa Bell in 1926. Yet the 'gamble' of a business that arose from the Woolfs' interest in printing, which Leonard developed in order to give Virginia a form of relaxation and alternative employment when the pressures of writing threatened her mental equilibrium, succeeded to such an extent that its story has been described by Nigel Nicolson as 'one of the legends of publishing'.

The beginnings were inauspicious. The Woolfs had no capital. They owned only a very simple printing machine which they operated in their dining-room. Their sitting-room served as their office. They had no experience in the actual production and promotion of books. The books they planned to publish were not recognisably saleable.

So why did they succeed? The explanation lies largely in Leonard's determination and in their choice of books. After the Hogarth Press's first book *Two Stories*, to which both Leonard and Virginia were contributors, their very earliest authors included Katherine Mansfield, T.S. Eliot and E.M. Forster, all hardly known at that stage. These were followed by novelists and poets equally little known such as Robert Graves, William Plomer, Cecil Day Lewis, Christopher Isherwood and, of course, Virginia Woolf herself. If to this significant list one adds authors such as Vita Sackville-West, Maynard Keynes, Roger Fry, Rose Macaulay and others; if one recognises the range of foreign writers translated and brought to British readers for the first time; if one appreciates the breadth of topics that were published, ranging through psychoanalysis, political thought, economics, music and others – then one can understand that the Hogarth Press made a most impressive contribution to English thought and literature in the years between the two world wars.

Roger Fry
Nina Hamnett Reading
(*c.*1917)
One of the most noted bohemians of the English art world, Nina Hamnett was painted and drawn by Fry on many occasions in 1917 – 18. Here he captures her cropped hair and distinctive profile.

OPPOSITE
Duncan Grant
Leonard Woolf (*c.*1912)

However, Leonard always contrived to keep the Hogarth Press small, and this was almost certainly an important ingredient in its success. Furthermore Leonard and Virginia maintained their personal involvement in every aspect of the business throughout the 1920s and 1930s. This is well illustrated in one of Virginia's incisive letters to a complaining customer.

Dear Madam,

As one of the guilty parties I bow down to your strictures upon the printing of 'On Being Ill'. I agree the colour is uneven, the letters not always clear, the spacing inaccurate, and the word 'campion' should read 'companion'. All I have to urge in excuse is that printing is a hobby carried on in the basement of a London house; that as amateurs all instruction in the art was denied us; that we have picked up what we know for ourselves; and that we practise printing in the intervals of lives that are otherwise engaged. In spite of all this, I believe that you can already sell your copy for more than the guinea you gave, as the edition is largely over subscribed, so that though we have not satisfied your taste, we hope we have not robbed your purse.

Yours, with apologies

Virginia Woolf

Vanessa Bell
Still Life with Wine Glass and Jug (c.1945)

Images of Virginia Woolf

Hermione Lee

Duncan Grant
Still Life: Coffee Table
(1914)
One of several similar paintings, all painted at Leonard
and Virginia Woolf's house
at Asheham near Lewes in
Sussex in the late summer
of 1914.

There are some images of Virginia Woolf which have powerfully fixed our perceptions of her. We all know the famous Beresford photograph of Virginia Stephen in her early twenties, which, in poster form, has been stuck up on the walls of so many devoted Woolfians. That image shows us how alluring and wistful she could appear. The sensual, down-curved lips, the large sad gazing eyes, the dark lashes and strong eyebrows, the lovely straight nose and delicate curve of the chin, the long elegant neck, the high cheekbones, the soft, loosely-coiled bun, the pretty ear lobe, and the ethereal lacy dress; these features, so often reproduced, have settled our idea of the delicate, unapproachable young virgin, which was to be so crucial in the forming of the Legend of Virginia as aetherial, otherworldly and fragile. That shy look askance was echoed many years later in the wonderful photograph of Virginia Woolf wearing her mother's dress which appeared in *Vogue* in 1926. But she didn't always look so vulnerable. Photographs of Virginia don't show a simple or a consistent per-sonality. In the bold Man Ray images of 1934, which show her made up, hair shining and smoothly centre parted, elegantly dressed, in cool, contained attitudes, we see an image of a woman of great powers, formidable intelligence and humour, and a daunting social presence, a woman used to exerting her will. Later photographs, again quite different, taken by Gisele Freund in 1939, show a face full of pain and deep thought, lovely and remote.

Virginia Woolf didn't want Freund to take those pictures, and she did not enjoy being paint-ed. She couldn't bear her sessions with the sculptor Stephen Tomlin, and Duncan Grant (according to Richard Shone) used to say that he could never get her to sit down and be used as a model. It is telling and true that the best-known painted image of her, by Vanessa, painted in 1912, sitting in a deckchair, has left the face blank, as though keeping its secrets and refusing to be pinned down.

OPPOSITE
Duncan Grant
Still Life: Vase of Flowers
(1914)
Grant painted figures on
either side of this vase in a
pottery in Tunis in early
1914, and this still life with
yellow tulips was probably
painted in Paris in May.

Vanessa Bell
Leonard Woolf (*c*.1940)
A study for the painting in
the National Portrait
Gallery, London.

That closed-off face, that refusal to be 'taken', is part of the challenge Virginia Woolf presents to her biographer. All readers of her diaries and letters will feel that they know her intimately and will want to call her 'Virginia'. But the more you find out about her the more reluctant you feel to sum her up. As she has Mrs Dalloway observe, 'She would not say of anyone in the world now that they were this or were that'. This is one of the most interesting paradoxes in Virginia Woolf. She is a great satirist with a wicked skill in caricature. She loves to catch people on paper or to put them down in public. She can be snobbish, critical and scornful. But she is also – and sometimes in the same breath – sympathetic, infinitely curious about other people, generous and desperately eager to get out of herself and into someone else's life. When I read through the hundreds of condolence letters written to Leonard after her death, the word most often used of her was 'kind'. It was not what I expected.

Almost all her writing is concerned with this doubleness: the desire to catch the essence of a self (she is fascinated by biography and what it can, and can't, do) and the recognition that – like her Lighthouse – nothing is ever 'one thing'. There is no one 'image' of Virginia Woolf. In the years since her death she has produced an amazing variety of different readings. Her story is reformulated by each generation of readers. So she is the difficult modernist preoccupied with questions of form, or the comedian of manners, or the neurotic highbrow aesthete, or the inventive fantasist, or the pernicious snob, or the Marxist feminist, or the lesbian heroine, or the cultural analyst – all depending on who is reading her and when and in what context. And the images which she produces and which are constructed for her will go on being argued about for many years to come, long after my book is published.

Duncan Grant
Fanny Reading (c.1962)
Angelica and David Garnett's daughter is here painted in Duncan Grant's studio at Charleston, sitting in a chair purchased from Heal's by Virginia Woolf and given by her to Vanessa Bell. The chair remains in Duncan Grant's studio at Charleston.

Maynard Keynes and The Creative Arts

Craufurd Goodwin

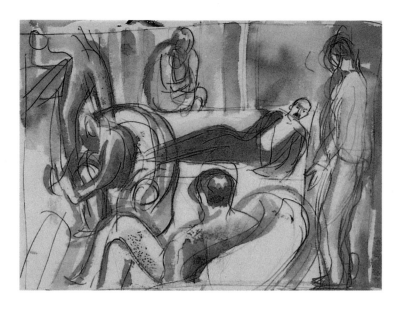

Not before John Maynard Keynes, and not since, has economic science been so intertwined with the creative arts. Keynes gave much to the arts, as friend, adviser and patron of Duncan Grant, Vanessa Bell and other Bloomsbury painters, as co-founder in 1925 of the London Artists' Association (like the Omega Workshops, an experiment of an artists' co-operative), as treasurer of the Camargo Society that attempted to establish an English ballet, and as moving force behind the establishment of the Cambridge Arts Theatre in 1934. Opinions differ about Keynes's taste in the arts, but all agree that his enthusiasm, enjoyment and commitment were intense.

Keynes took from the arts at least as much as he gave to them. Above all, in his economic theory he joined in the spirit of rebellion and experimentation that was a character of Bloomsbury. It was his disciples, not he, who spoke of the 'Keynesian Revolution', but he took pains to distinguish himself from his predecessors, not only the classical economists of the eighteenth and nineteenth centuries, but even his own mentor, Alfred Marshall, and Marshall's successor at Cambridge, Arthur Pigou. As a declaration of independence from predecessors, Keynes's *General Theory of Employment, Interest and Money* has parallels with Lytton Strachey's *Eminent Victorians* and Roger Fry's *Vision and Design*.

Three aspects of Keynes's economics bear close relationships to the creative arts of Bloomsbury and to the wider intellectual life of Britain in his time. First, he was unhappy with the portrayal of human behaviour embodied in conventional market models. Humans, he was convinced, were more complex and interesting than the rationally calculating utility maximisers described by that quintessentially Victorian social theorist Leslie Stephen, father of Vanessa Bell and Virginia Woolf, in his study *The English Utilitarians*. In his search for a

Vanessa Bell
Lydia Lopokova (1927)
One of several studies
Vanessa Bell made of the
Russian ballerina and her
husband Maynard Keynes.
The final painting portrayed
Lopokova dancing in a ver-
sion of the Can-Can from
La Boutique Fantasque
with Keynes looking from
behind the curtain.

richer understanding of human behaviour, Keynes was much influenced by the new ethics of
G.E. Moore, and he was aware, at least at second hand from James and Alix Strachey, of
developments in Freudian psychology. Perhaps from his exposure to the writers of Bloomsbury
he came to appreciate the complexity of human behaviour and was led to probe the springs
of human action in his own remarkable *Essays in Biography*. He did not pose any simple alternative to utility maximisation as an explanation for human action but he remained fascinated
with the mercurial character of his fellow investors in capital markets, upon which, he
concluded, prosperity of the economy ultimately depended. He spoke of 'animal spirits' to
characterise some market behaviour, a term that has a distinctly Bloomsbury ring.

The single idea for which Keynes is most remembered is that unemployment can emerge, and may persist, in a free-market economy and that unemployment can be alleviated with relative ease by an enlightened governmental spending programme to create jobs. Full and efficient use of national resources had been the main objective of economists long before Keynes. But he was exceptional in recognising the distinctly human costs of unemployment; to lose a job is to lose dignity, a sense of self-worth, a place in society. It is reasonable to conclude that Keynes's sensitivity to unemployment was heightened by his association with the artists of Bloomsbury and beyond, a milieu with whom other economists had far less intimate contact. Take E.M. Forster, Keynes's colleague at King's College, as a case in point. In *Howard's End*, Leonard Bast's unemployment is caused by the casual actions of the thoughtless entrepreneur, Henry Willcox. Then the fumbling philanthropic efforts of Willcox's sister-in-law, Helen, only make the matter worse. The outcome is Bast's death. The conclusion that Forster's reader must reach is that nothing less than society acting collectively and compassionately could have saved Leonard Bast. This, of course, was the conclusion of Keynes's economics as well.

Since Keynes's death in 1946, economics has moved away once more from the creative arts – to the impoverishment of both.

Roger Fry
Near Murcia, Spain (1933)
In a letter of 18 April 1933 to Gerald Brenan, Fry wrote 'Did I tell you that I got my sketch of the pass between Cartagena and Murcia? It is one of the best I did'.

Frances: The Boswell of Bloomsbury

Nigel Nicolson

Duncan Grant
Lydia Dancing (c.1920)
Lydia Lopokova was
acclaimed as 'London's
favourite ballerina' because
of her enormous vitality
and comic gifts. Here Grant
has drawn her in *Scotch
Reel*.

OPPOSITE
Vanessa Bell
Faith Henderson (c.1917)
Frances Partridge has said
that Faith Henderson was
sometimes known as the
'Chinless Wonder'; this
aspect of her features is evident here. Faith was the
wife of Hubert Henderson,
appointed by Keynes to be
the editor of the *Nation
and Athenaeum*.

A very old woman (she would recoil at being called a lady, but she is one) sits at a table in The Bloomsbury Workshop, a book-and-art shop near the British Museum, signing copies of the latest volume of her diary. She is ninety-eight years old.

She is often described as the last survivor of the Bloomsbury Group, but wrongly, for we still have with us at this date George Rylands, and Angelica Garnett, who was ostensibly the daughter of Clive Bell, but actually of Duncan Grant. It is typical of Bloomsbury frankness about such matters that in the index to Frances Partridge's *Life Regained* she is listed as '*née* Grant'.

Frances Partridge was the loveliest of the Bloomsbury girls. She did not scintillate; that was not her style. She was intelligent, attentive, alert, immensely companionable, and 'nice' in a competitive world of intellectuals where niceness was suspect and the word itself was taboo. She grew in harmony as she grew in years. Today she is fragile, but with a vitality that makes any attempt to help her, or remind her of whom one is, almost an impertinence.

It was not until she was seventy-five that she discovered that in this company of writers she had been a writer too. She had kept a diary for most of her life, and in 1978 began to publish it. It describes the travels, loves, thoughts and relationships of a small group of friends, mostly second- or third-generation Bloomsbury. She is their Boswell. It is excellently done.

There are constant reminders of Bloomsbury's great days. Strangers have asked her what Dora Carrington was like, whether Lytton Strachey ever lost his temper, and patiently she replies. 'It is quite extraordinary,' she wrote in 1971, 'what power to grip people's imagination the old, old story contains,' and she was central to that story.

Dora Carrington
Julia Strachey (c.1925)
A portrait of Lytton
Strachey's neice, who married Stephen Tomlin. She
wrote *Cheerful Weather for
the Wedding*, published by
the Hogarth Press, and is
the subject of Frances
Partridge's book *Julia*.

She has been infuriated by the prejudice that lingered, and still lingers, about the Bloomsbury Group. When a literary editor said to her: 'They were all just dolls; nothing to them at all. No one cares about anything they did,' Frances replied quietly, but with devastating effect, 'You mean Maynard's and Virginia's achievements are worthless?' and she could have named others: Fry, Eliot, Forster, Strachey, Leonard Woolf, the Bells.

There has not been a set of friends whose influence has been so pervasive since Dr Johnson's coterie died out. To give but one example: their attitude to women. They took the cause of feminism for granted. People are people of different types, and among those types are male and female, a distinction which, except biologically, is not of great importance. Women should be valued for what they are, for what they have to contribute. That was a rare assumption eighty years ago.

Today we know more about the Bloomsberries than they knew about each other. That may be one of the troubles: we know too much. Their gossip, their infidelities, their ambitions, vanities and failures have been totally exposed for our inspection in their published letters, diaries and reminiscences. They are regarded as self-satisfied, snobbish and boring, even by so humane a man as Bernard Levin.

Why should this be so? I suspect that it is symptomatic of the British delight in cutting intellectuals down to size, and our contempt for scholarship, like the pleasure we took in the revelation that 'Piltdown Man' was nothing but an ape's skull.

The Americans have shown Bloomsbury greater respect. Our Virginia has become their Woolf. It was only in 1998 that a British society was formed in her name, to study her life and works, and it set itself the unambitious target of 200 members.

Of all the Bloomsbury legacies, the greatest is their concept of friendship. Nothing – not age, nor success, nor rivalry in art and love, nor separation for long periods by war, travel or careers – ever parted these people who came together when they were young. Frances Partridge was one of them, and the record she has left behind deserves our gratitude.

Duncan Grant
Standing Woman (c.1956)
A study for Grant's mural decorations for the Russell Chantry, Lincoln Cathedral. The model is Angelica Garnett.

Omega

Quentin Bell

I n the summer of 1916, when the Omega Workshops were already ailing but still in existence, Duncan Grant, Vanessa Bell and others were in Suffolk, growing fruit and vegetables, raising poultry, and attempting to avoid military service. It was the poultry that led to trouble; they began to vanish mysteriously. They were white birds (Leghorns?) with red combs; so too were the fowls of our next-door neighbours, and as our flock diminished, theirs seemed to increase. It was, I think, Duncan who took a bowl of blue dye and painted the rumps of our chickens. They looked very pretty, and we claimed also that their tricoloured look was patriotic. Our neighbours thought otherwise: that chickens should have blue tails seemed to them an affront to nature; they suspected us of mocking the flag, and charged us with suggesting that they were dishonest.

In its way the incident was typical of that period. It was a time when artists would paint anything; not only pictures but pots, chairs, hats, fabrics and, at a pinch, poultry. They continued to paint what they saw but what they saw they also painted; to adapt a phrase of Karl Marx: 'For them it was not sufficient to depict the world, but to change it'.

'A bunch of amateurs', complained those who had been reared in the sober and exact disciplines of the crafts. 'Your rickety chairs,' they said, 'will come to grief even before the paint that you have daubed on them peels off.'

'Alas,' muttered the artists, 'if only one could say the same of *your* furniture.'

Both sides had a case: well-made things are not always beautiful, and Omega things are not always well made (although here I must say that having sat, lounged, lolled and boisterously

Vanessa Bell
Omega Paintpots (1915)
A painting given by Vanessa Bell to Winifred Gill, one of her fellow artists at the Omega Workshops, and eventually its manager.

OPPOSITE
Vanessa Bell
The Virgin in Prayer (1917)
The reinterpretation by contemporary artists of old master paintings was the theme of one of the exhibitions organised by Fry at the Omega Workshops. Here Vanessa Bell has given Sassoferrato's figure a strikingly coloured face and veil.

Duncan Grant
Decorative Panel (1950s)
It is possible that this may
have been a design for a
door.

laughed on Omega chairs – and some of us weighed sixteen stone and more – I saw those chairs stand up to vile usage for over half a century at Charleston). Today those arguments are for the most part of purely historical interest, but that interest is considerable and, although it has been considered by persons better equipped than I am, it seems worth pointing out that this sudden incursion of 'fine artists' into the domain of the craftsman was something rather new in the history of European art. Hitherto the art of the academies – that which was known as 'high art' – had dissociated itself, not without a certain *hauteur*, from the business of the craftsmen, the rude mechanics, and when art schools began to be established in this country considerable fears were voiced that these might train students for work above their station. It took an industrial revolution to persuade the public that any kind of art education should be provided to serve industry, and it was in this country that the first attempts were made to unite the work of the fine artists with that of the ornamentalists. It was here too that in *le style anglais* the century was given an ornamental language of its own.

Meanwhile in France the innovators remained entirely concerned with the observation of nature, and I doubt whether the Impressionists ever got any further in the direction of ornamental art than the painting of a fan.

Nevertheless it was in France that the followers of Cézanne and later the innovators of the twentieth century developed a style which was largely removed from the observation of nature, and it was this which lay ready to hand when Roger Fry created the Omega Workshops.

OPPOSITE
Roger Fry
Red Hot Pokers (c.1916)
The painting shows a vase,
small bowl and plate all
made by Fry for the Omega
Workshops.

Was it really like this? Not altogether; the proximate reason for their creation was Roger Fry's discovery that this was the only way in which young and penniless artists could be given a living wage. It was the fact that Duncan Grant could not find the money to take him from London to visit Roger at Guildford which launched the movement. But the underlying reasons were to be found in the development of capitalist society. It was these which in the end moved the painters to decorate tables, chairs, pots, hats – and poultry.

Vanessa Bell

Anne Olivier Bell

I t was through Helen Anrep that I first met – or at first didn't meet – my future mother-in-law, Vanessa Bell. I had run into Helen's son Igor with his friends Bill Coldstream and Graham Bell at the 1937 Paris exhibition *Chefs d'Oeuvres de l'Art Français*; they took me along to the Hôtel de Londres as they were to dine with Igor's mother. Coming down the stairs, Mrs Anrep halted us; and we observed in the hall below a group of three figures forming as it were a bodyguard to a fourth – a tall, stooping, infinitely sad-looking grey lady. This was Vanessa. It was some two months after the death in Spain of her beloved son Julian, and Duncan Grant and her other two children had brought her to Paris to see the exhibition.

I saw a good deal of Helen Anrep in subsequent years and often stayed with her in her Suffolk home. She would frequently speak of her intimate friend Vanessa Bell, always emphasising however what a *private* person she was, so I never actually met her until some years after the war when I was working in the Arts Council. Helen had a drinks party at her flat in Percy Street, and here at last I was introduced to Vanessa. Given Helen's warnings, I was surprised by Vanessa's ease and charm of manner and her affability, and overcome when she asked if I would come for a weekend to Charleston and sit for a large painting she was to do (willing sitters were hard to come by in the country). I went, of course, but with considerable trepidation. Clive Bell, Duncan Grant and Quentin were all there. I was greatly relieved that little was expected of me in this supposed HQ of Bloomsbury intellectualism beyond listening politely, sitting to be painted and luxuriating in Charleston's summer magic.

Well reader, in due course I married Quentin. I remember at Charleston shortly before the ceremony (due to take place on a day which was hijacked for the funeral of King George VI and thus deemed by the Registrar 'unsuitable' for weddings), Vanessa asking Quentin after

Vanessa Bell
Olivier Bell (1952)
Reclining with a book on the sofa (formerly owned by Walter Sickert) in Duncan Grant's studio, Quentin's wife is clearly pregnant with their first child, Julian.

OPPOSITE
Vanessa Bell
Self Portrait (c.1952)
This introspective painting with facial features obscured is one of around six self portraits painted by Vanessa Bell in the last decade of her life. All of those self portraits, as Richard Shone has noted, 'purvey a sense of isolation'.

dinner if he had remembered the wedding ring. Ah, no. Well, she thought she might supply one; and from a jewel box produced several possible items, one of which was seized by Duncan, exclaiming that it was his mother's. However, a delicate gold band engraved with the words 'Le Coeur le Donne' was chosen; it had been prepared for George Duckworth's intended bride – but she had broken the engagement. I had no idea who George Duckworth was.

Although our marriage removed Quentin from Charleston where he had seemed an irreplaceable mediating presence in that ageing household, we were able regularly to spend long periods there during university holidays. Mealtimes were the principal occasions for interaction between all the inhabitants. Breakfast in this respect was a non-starter – independent arrivals (often with reading matter), independent tastes – Duncan had proper porridge with SALT; eggs, bacon, etc. were keeping warm on or in the Aga in the kitchen; toast and marmalade; the unifying emotion was WAITING FOR THE POST. When it came, Clive would appropriate *The Times*, Duncan and Vanessa, given favourable weather, would stroll on to the gravel before the house and discuss their letters (if any), their plans for the day, or consider the garden – ought they to order bulbs, wouldn't it be a good idea were they to plant a hibiscus/a tree peony/some tiger lilies … At one o'clock Grace rang the handbell in the hall; lunch was usually cold meat, salad, cheese and beer. Not much conversation: local gossip – Mr Stevens the ancient gardener; Mr Bush the Gage Estate Agent – a nice man but an inevitable target for abuse; the deficiencies of the water supply. Five o'clock: tea time – proper tea with bread and jam and home-made cake. Vanessa would sometimes come down early from her attic studio and with what seemed to me extraordinary speed and sang-froid, make scones for tea.

Duncan Grant
Helen Anrep in the Garden, Charleston (c.1942)
Helen Anrep lived with Roger Fry in his last years. After Fry's death she remained a good friend of Duncan Grant and Vanessa Bell and she features in several of their drawings and paintings.

The Charleston dining-table being round, there was no head to it; but Vanessa was the head. She carved, distributed the food, poured the tea, presided. The evening meal, always beginning with soup, followed by flesh or fowl and pudding, with wine at weekends, was the occasion for real Conversation – conversation which was stylish, brilliant, funny, informed, wide ranging, and carried on rather in the manner of a tennis match, batted to and fro across the table. This was principally led by Clive (on the best French model), whose strokes were skilfully returned by Quentin; Duncan would sometimes sneak in a drop shot, while Vanessa on the whole was an indulgent umpire, limiting herself to observations on the

Vanessa Bell
Decorative Design (*c*.1933)

Duncan Grant
Vanessa Bell (c.1917)

absurdity of the protagonists. (I was ball-boy and as insignificant as possible.) After dinner we moved to the sitting-room, where Vanessa poured coffee, and the conversation match would continue: art and literature, history and philosophy. Vanessa invariably but entirely inconspicuously fell asleep in her chair; waking equally inconspicuously some time later, she was likely to observe, 'What nonsense you all talk'. When Clive had finished his cigar and his interest in the subject under discussion, he would get up and go off to bed; Quentin, who was an early riser, soon followed; and I, who was a night bird, stayed put. Vanessa and Duncan then began to talk easily and comfortably on a quite different level – gossip, news of the granddaughters, news of friends, possible visitors and arrangements, Grace's foibles, Duncan's movements – a sort of simple talk with which I felt quite at home and could join. Vanessa occasionally made references to her life as a young lady in Kensington, and it is one of my great regrets that knowing as I then did *nothing* of that incongruous world in which she had been brought up, I was unable to draw her out to talk of it – which I am sure she would have been happy to do.

In the ten years that I knew her Vanessa was always wonderful to me – wonderful in my eyes and wonderful towards me – and not only because I provided her with three more grandchildren to adore.

Vanessa Bell
Girls doing Needlework
(*c*.1928 – 30)
This quick sketch shows
Angelica Bell (*right*) and
Judith Bagenal, either
painted at Charleston or at
Cassis in France.

The Pond

Angelica Garnett

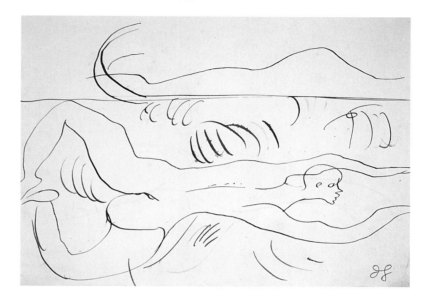

Duncan Grant
Swimmer (*c.*1916)

On seeing the pond for the first time in 1916 Vanessa came away with the impression that it was a lake. This at least is how the family understood her references to it. Although she was afterwards laughed at for magnifying its size, for seeing it as something out of all proportion to our style of life or to the fact that Charleston was not a mansion but an ordinary farmhouse, it remained in my mind *her* pond, even her lake – a symbol or, better still, a mirage we lived with and which became for each of us all-important. We could, as Virginia would have said, boast that, although many farms have or had ponds, ours was bigger than most. And it is to this dignity that the pond has now been restored.

Had Charleston not had its pond it would have been like any other farm stranded, after centuries of unremitting labour, among the dry furrows of the uplands. But the pond, over and above its practical uses, saved it from such, together with its red-tiled dormer-windowed roof, so typical of Sussex. It also mirrored the dream that someone had once had, by planting the occasional laurel bush on the slope in front of the house, of conferring on it some notion of bourgeois conventionality. Seen from the dining-room window, this may have lulled the ego of those who lived there into thinking they were, socially speaking, on the up and up.

For before we lived there Charleston had been a boarding house. Previous owners had a punt on the pond which we inherited. There is at least one photograph of the punt, steered by the half-naked, aboriginal figure of my brother Julian, for whom the pond encapsulated the world of nature, as yet tranquil and unviolated. It was a kingdom he ruled over with a certain careless arrogance, a dream that lay between earth and sky, suggestive of further horizons. Had he lived longer he might have written a poem about it.

OPPOSITE

Vanessa Bell
The Garden at Charleston
(*c.*1945)

At its edge, Julian and Quentin spent hours chiselling with their penknives into huge lumps of chalk brought from the quarry in the Downs, which they transformed into castles. Penetrated by holes and passages, these would disgorge armies of scarlet berries which attacked or defended or were conquered – betraying an obsession with war natural enough for children of the twentieth century.

However, despite their thoughts of war, the pond itself reflected the extraordinary, apparently unlimited peace of those years. For me, excluded from such games mainly because I was that ambiguous quantity, a (very) young female, separated from them also by the rules of nursery life, the water simply spelt wonder. I looked into it and through it, hardly knowing but not caring who I was or how I fitted in. The pond was a boon, a gift which contained the mystery of being different. This was its fascination while, at the same time, it meant little, since there was no problem for me in becoming a fish, a frog or even a waterweed. It was thus I made friends with the pond, and thus I saw it as an extension of Vanessa, whose huge grey eyes absorbed its image as she stood on the bank, moving her brush like an antenna over the surface of her canvas.

It was of course the painters for whom the pond existed in every dimension. Seen from within as part of the house, or from without as a purely abstract, significant form, it played its role over and over again on their canvases. They stood in quiet corners, indefatigably analysing the pond's appearance – cool in the mornings, or glowing in the long shadows of the evening.

But in Duncan's active imagination it was also an opportunity to fantasise. His vision, composed mostly of pictorial memories such as wall paintings from Pompeii, saw pagodas and flamingos as part of our landscape. He even went as far as making enquiries about flamingos in some bird sanctuary. Laughed at for his unpracticality, he did in the end succeed in erecting a construction called a gazebo on the far side of the pond. Sitting on it one could stare at the duckweed and watch the dragonflies, or the horses and cows as they came down to drink in the evening. Made of thin slats of wood, the gazebo did not, however, last for more than a year or two.

The nineteenth of August was Quentin's birthday, an occasion for fireworks. For tea there was a birthday cake and then a fine dinner with grouse, sent from Scotland by Clive's brother Cory. Afterwards the smell of brandy and cigars would fill the interval while we waited for the streaks of sunset to disappear from the pond's surface. Meanwhile the boys were busy planting their catherine wheels and rockets under the willow tree, full of the excitement of doing and organising things on their own. Finally the show started and I, wrapped in a shawl and half asleep, would be seized by the whooshing sound of a rocket, alarmed for an instant and then enchanted by the slow, silent descent of its red and blue stars reflected, for good measure, in the water.

One year there was a drought. The stream which fed the pond dried up and the perennial leak widened. The water evaporated, leaving an expanse of clay, cracked like the craters of the moon, and covered with dead duckweed under which flipped the slow-dying fish. Our summer, unrefreshed, became stale and unprofitable.

Vanessa Bell
Spring Flowers (c. 1950)

At first the pond was a responsibility shared between ourselves and the farmer. He used it and we enjoyed it, contributing when necessary to its upkeep. But when, eventually, the horses became redundant and the cows were watered in their parlour, the farmer paid the pond no more attention. In the 1970s when Duncan, the only survivor of the older generation, kept almost open house at Charleston it became clear that one of his elegant ideas had been regrettable: the pond had become choked with bulrushes. An army of friends was mobilised and descended almost naked into the mud, to pull out armfuls of the offending plant hoping, at the end of the day, to reveal a clear patch of water. The effort was heroic. The sun shone and the pleasure of watching half-naked figures bearing swathes of drooping rushes was a sight in the purest Charleston tradition. As an operation however it was not totally successful. It was only when the Charleston Trust took it over that the pond regained a purity that never belonged to it in our day. Now it has been furnished with fish and plants and represents a miraculous survival. It has again a life of its own. The only things lacking are the children who once took it so much for granted.

Vanessa Bell
Charleston Pond (1920)
One of sixteen watercolours
that Vanessa Bell exhibited
in 1920 at the Independent
Gallery, London, in which
her co-exhibitors were
Duncan Grant and Robert
Lotiron.

The Myths and Fantasies of Duncan Grant

Richard Shone

Duncan Grant
Venus on a Couch (c.1919)
One of several studies pre-
liminary to Grant's well-
known painting *Venus and
Adonis* in the Tate, London.

I think it was Duncan Grant's early study of Poussin's drawings in the Louvre that formed the basis for his calligraphic wizardry over a world of nymphs and satyrs and sporting gods and goddesses. His sketchbooks from then onwards (c.1906 – 7) brim with such figures. Although he rarely stresses a particular narrative, he certainly had his favourite moments – Venus languishing while Adonis hunts, Europa, breeze-swept on her maritime bull, Daphne pursued by Apollo (the subject of a beautiful textile design), Narcissus contemplating his reflection, Psyche lifting her lamp to look more closely at the sleeping Amor. In old age he continued to delight in the Greek and Roman myths and in Ovid's *Metamorphoses*. By then they had taken on a patina from his reading of the Elizabethan poets and his love of Purcell and Blow, Handel and Gluck, as well as his profound admiration for Titian.

When it came to painting such scenes himself, however, the results were curious. At an earlier period he could produce the striking *Venus and Adonis* (c.1919, Tate Gallery) or the *Nymph and Satyr* (c.1925). Later, his heavier, more laborious handling of paint seemed to obstruct his natural fantasy, and the loosely draped figures of his imagined world danced with feet of clay. The oil sketch for *Venus at her Toilet* (for Penns-in-the-Rocks) is infinitely lighter and lovelier than the grand but stilted final version (in Southampton Art Gallery). But the preliminary sketches on paper continually remind us both of the ease with which he enters this idealised realm and of his corresponding fluency of line, as though it sprang from his fingertips uninflected by day-to-day realities.

Classic myths and legends, their protagonists spurred by mortal love and tinged with melancholy transience, were far closer to Duncan Grant's heartbeat than Biblical stories and the New Testament, though he found congenial subjects there throughout his life. One of his last figure paintings was a *Garden of Gethsemane*. But there is an almost mischievous element in his sleeping naked figures, easily mistaken for the post-coital slumbering of untroubled Greek gods.

Duncan Grant
Acrobat (c.1960)

The Art of Dora Carrington

Jane Hill

The question I am most often asked about my work on *The Art of Dora Carrington* is what attracted me to her. It was always an easy question to answer. For the girl of twenty-one that I then was, the serendipitous discovery of Carrington's published letters and extracts from her diaries seemed like a gift. I felt I understood what motivated Carrington and what guided her. I even thought if I had known this person we would have been friends.

I was enthralled by her quirkiness; the look of her, her wit, her eclectic taste, her way of seeing and, what was clear from her painterly, illuminating letters, that she was first and foremost an artist, constantly conceiving ideas for paintings and plucking visions from the air. But where were these pictures? In 1987 there was only one painting to be seen in a public collection and that was of E.M. Forster at the National Portrait Gallery, London. Most of the rest were privately owned.

When I started touring the country, cataloguing Carrington's work and meeting her family and friends, I was touched by the living affection, and amazed by how extraordinarily vital – considering Carrington had died in 1932 – their memories were. Rosamond Lehmann said of Carrington: 'I still think of her as the closest friend I ever had. She was one of the most unboring people I ever knew and I miss her very much, still.' And when I visited Carrington's last lover, the taciturn Beakus Penrose down in Cornwall, I found his home spoke volumes; it proved his strong aesthetic sense and hinted at his appeal for Carrington. Her enigmatic paintings hung in every house I visited and presided over our hospitable, fireside chats. It helped to piece together the patchwork.

Dora Carrington
Woman Walking Away (c.1914)

My desire to achieve a sense of time, culture and place also took me on a Quixotic journey to Spain in search of Gerald Brenan's 'yellow oxhide land' which had inspired Carrington's unearthly Yegen 'landscape'. A granddaughter of Robert Graves, who I'd been introduced to by a mutual friend, led me down a precipitous path, improbably planted with waving, blue, sentinel flag irises, to a small stone house with an English garden, perched on the side of a ravine in the Alpujarras. It was lived in by one of Augustus John's grandchildren, who had also built it, and we drank tea out of fine china whilst he played Mozart on the piano. He, in turn, took me to Lynda Nicholson Price, the poet who had worked with Brenan in his late years on *St John of the Cross*. Researching my book has been one happy discovery after another, often of things that I was not always aware I was in quest of; and in search of Carrington's life I discovered my own.

Myths and thorny gardens abound around Carrington – not least the romantic legend of her 'Triangular Trinity of Happiness' with Lytton Strachey and her husband Ralph Partridge – often obscuring her very real, albeit quietly made achievements. Carrington's life was rich in personal associations but she remained an isolated worker and, because she practised her art so privately, she has until now had only a modest recognition of her contribution to modern British painting. But Carrington had a streak of creative genius; there was an immense range to her art and she worked unremittingly throughout her short life, faithful to her own distinctive voice, which was more akin to the English pastoral and popular tradition than to the Post-Impressionism of her peers.

Carrington's guiding lights were her passion for 'people and paint'. Purpose, in Carrington's life, became inextricably bound up in her companion and love, Lytton Strachey. When Lytton died Carrington's own lights went out. The major retrospective of Carrington's work and the film *Carrington* written by Christopher Hampton and featuring Emma Thompson illustrates that interest in Carrington is waxing not waning. The Bloomsbury Workshop, which once provided me with a base for my own research on Carrington, offers a rare opportunity to see a combination of Carrington's sketchbook drawings and a few kindly loaned watercolours and oils. These highlight Carrington's appeal as an artist, notwithstanding the affection she inspired as a person both in her lifetime and subsequently.

Dora Carrington
Samuel Carrington
(*c*.1914)
As Jane Hill has noted,
'Carrington was devoted to
her father and loved to
draw him'.

Janie Bussy

Angelica Garnett

Duncan Grant
Julian Bell (c.1930)
A drawing of Clive and
Vanessa Bell's son Julian
(1908 – 37).

Calling Janie to mind is for me as easy as switching on the electric light – as easy as though I had seen her yesterday, very probably because I possess a marvellous and delicate portrait of her in pastel by her father, Simon Bussy. Its subtlety and purity were surely the result of his daughter's personality, into which, both as portraitist and father, he must have seen as deeply as anyone. Drawn when she was nineteen or twenty years old, it represents the full face of a young woman still in thrall to the dreams of childhood, whose struggle to free herself would never perhaps quite succeed.

The Janie I recall is however of a later date and, though recognisably the same, rather different. Slim and slightly curved, like the stem of a tall glass, I see her sitting on a deckchair on the lawn at Charleston. Her back is cradled by the canvas of the chair, while her long elegant legs in high-heeled sandals are crossed in an unconscious gesture of self protection, and a book half falls from narrow, fastidious hands. In a gauche way she was, I think, sexy, but her sensuality, detectable in the droop of her scarlet lips, remained unsatisfied. Her bobbed hair, straight as a die and cut to a point in the nape of her neck, swung over the eyes, and it was these that fascinated. Almond shaped, they would change at any moment from glowing charcoal to the glint of anthracite, critical or brooding according to the mood of the moment.

OPPOSITE

Roger Fry
Angles-sur-L'Anglin (1912)
One of several paintings
executed by Fry of a pictur-
esque spot near Poitiers in
France which he visited by
bicycle with Clive Bell and
Duncan Grant towards the
end of 1911.

Precariously balanced between France and England, spending six months of the year in each country, she may have suffered from a feeling of not belonging entirely to either, but the enforced duality certainly enriched her life and personality. Highly cultivated, she was always aware of what was going on both socially and politically, and carried her background with her. Her Frenchness, a quality for which all the members of my family were suckers, was for us like a whiff of strong brandy, while her many French friends appreciated her intimate knowledge of the English scene, its history, literature and poetry.

Her parents had made a romantic marriage. Dorothy Strachey was descended from an ancient patrician family, intellectual and unpractical, while Simon was the son and grandson of shoemakers, a profession linked to the earth and to the peasants who wore their shoes. On hearing that her daughter intended to marry Simon, Lady Strachey drew attention to the fact that he mopped up his gravy with a morsel of bread. She was hardly pleased to find herself expected to welcome as son-in-law the small, gruff but intensely sensitive fellow who, besides being an exceptionally gifted painter, was also a skilful gardener and discriminating gourmet. His nature was uncompromising and passionate – a quality that may in the end have appealed to her as they did to Dorothy, herself a passionate puritan.

Janie's health was fragile and she was educated by Dorothy, attaining a degree of familiarity with the literature and art of both countries that put me to shame, Quentin and Julian certainly less so although, judging by Janie's sophistication, their development must have been far behind hers. She was however never arrogant or self-satisfied, and laced her knowledge with plenty of laughter which, transformed by chronic bronchitis, sounded like the croak of a tree frog. Her speaking voice, mostly a low, warm burr, would in excitement mount in pitch like that of all Stracheys.

Spending, as they did, the winter months in Roquebrune within sight of the Mediterranean, it was spring when the Bussys at last appeared in London with the swallows. Thus I saw Janie mostly at Charleston in the long summer holidays when she would arrive dressed with a frugal French elegance which, not having much money, she had no doubt searched for painstakingly. Her unerring taste, seen in the fine linen of her skirts, the coloured scarf round her neck, impressed my budding femininity. She knew, evidently, how to compensate for her 'laideur' even if she could not quite forget it.

For Quentin she was a friend whose background, although similar, was also sufficiently different to be stimulating, adding the difference of sex to a cultural affinity. For Julian I have heard that Janie entertained deeper feelings – but I do not know if they were reciprocated. She had in fact fallen in love with Trotsky – a convenient way of marking her interest in politics while playing a role which suited her gentle but maverick personality. Her conversations with Quentin, to which I often lent half an ear, were based on the art of teasing. They tickled each other with straws and arrived at no conclusions.

For me, in spite of twelve years difference in age, she tried hard to be an elder sister – and was in fact a second cousin. She allowed me to monopolise her for our amateur theatricals, playing the part of an American tourist in Quentin's prophetic charade of a future Charleston open to the public, and as a shepherd dressed in a sheet in one of my own less witty confections.

But if she listened gracefully enough to Clive's rather masturbatory accounts of his French adventures, and laughed lightly at Duncan's sallies, it was with Vanessa that Janie showed a deeper receptivity, responding to a maternal tenderness which liberated something in her that was more human, less brittle and defensive. They did not necessarily say much to each other although, for all I know, they may have indulged in private midnight intimacies, but

Vanessa no doubt understood Janie's longing for love and wished perhaps that she could have her as a daughter-in-law. At the same time she sympathised with her as a painter, whose art was by no means a mere imitation of her father's or that of her neighbours Zoum and Jean Vanden Eckhoudt or, for that matter, of Matisse, Simon's lifelong friend. Its transparence, brilliance and freshness may have taken something from each but was also of its time. Surrounded by these giants Janie floated under her own small and individual banner.

No one could have been more aware of the value of happiness, or of the fact that such happiness was mostly to be had from the exercise of common sense and thinking of other people. At the same time it was evident that she was aware of emotional undercurrents too strong for expression, and in the end her own life, far from being that of the modern young women she appeared to epitomise, resembled that of the Victorian spinster made hostage to her parents. If both Dorothy and Simon, like two strange birds sitting on the same branch, watched their chick develop with an intense and loving eye, jealous perhaps of her squandering gifts and qualities in strange places, they had no need to worry. Janie never left home, seeming to find enough spiritual nourishment within it and with her friends. By a sad accident she died at too early an age, just before her mother, whose death would, at least superficially, have liberated her lively and life-enhancing nature.

Roger Fry
Auxerre (1925)
An ink study for this painting is to be found at Charleston. Writing to Vanessa Bell at the time he painted this picture, Fry described how 'the town builds itself up rather theatrically over the Yonne with two huge Gothic churches dominating all. They're so magnificently placed and so frighteningly successful from a dramatic point of view that I rather succumb to them . . . .'

Vanessa Bell: Experiences of Paris Cafés

James Beechey

Vanessa Bell
Man Reading in a Paris Café (1920s)
Bordering on caricature, this is one of Vanessa's many drawings from life produced in Continental cafés.

In April 1904, in the aftermath of their father's death, Thoby Stephen and his sisters took a leisurely holiday through Italy. En route home to London they stopped off in Paris, where Thoby's Cambridge friend Clive Bell was living, profitably wasting his days studying the Old Masters in the Louvre and the new ones at the Luxembourg, making his first acquaintance of artists and writers, and embarking on a lifelong love affair with the French capital. Clive entertained his guests in Montparnasse where he had lodgings. He was pleased to show off his new surroundings and took them to his friends' studios and to local cafés. At the Chat Blanc they stayed talking and smoking until half-past eleven: a real Bohemian party, Virginia thought. She delighted in her first taste of café society – the memory of it remained particularly powerful and she perfectly evoked it twenty years later in *Jacob's Room*. Vanessa was perhaps even more enchanted and wrote to Clive from London that 'we have been horrifying George [Duckworth] with accounts of our doings at cafés and elsewhere'.

Clive and Vanessa Bell went occasionally to Paris after their marriage – they spent part of their honeymoon there in the spring of 1907 and dined at Le Petit Avenue with Duncan Grant – but it was only in the 1920s that they started to make regular visits separately or together. Montparnasse was still their quarter, though its character had quite changed from 1904 when Clive had offered Vanessa her first glimpse of it. In the immediate years before the war it had been colonised by the avant-garde and had become famously the epitome of artistic Paris. Clive Bell's first rooms there had overlooked a small, scruffy bistro, the Dôme, which did little business (not much later two students, Duncan Grant and Wyndham Lewis, would breakfast there together). Within a few years it had expanded down the street and flaunted its success on the pavements. The café life of Montparnasse was now essential to the legend of modern art, and at the tables of the Rotonde or the Select or the Deux Magots

OPPOSITE
Duncan Grant
Vanessa Bell (c.1916)

85

one might meet (and Bloomsbury often did) Picasso, Derain and Braque and their wives, Max Jacob or André Salmon and a host of lesser names.

Away from home, Vanessa Bell enjoyed a less hectic pace of life and she would linger happily in her favourite cafés – the Deux Magots, or the Régence, which Clive had been introduced to years earlier by the Canadian painter J.W. Morrice – sipping coffee, waiting for friends, making plans for that day and the next. Eventually the urge to preserve the scene would overcome her. Her daughter Angelica remembers that hours were spent there looking, watching and often secretly sketching under the table, so as neither to offend nor provoke unwanted interest. Tiny sketchbooks were filled with rapid portraits in thick black pencil, of heads and bodies, expressing Vanessa's wonder at the variety yet sameness of humanity and the humour with which she regarded it. Although café interiors – which gave the opportunity for tackling ambitious conversation pieces – were frequently the subject of paintings by younger artists who were friends of Bloomsbury, including Victor Pasmore and Edward Le Bas, I know of none by Vanessa Bell. But the drawings from Paris (and those also made surreptitiously in the cafés of Madrid, Rome and Venice) are just as telling of her absorption in the visual world, and are a reminder, too, of her particular gift for caricature.

Quentin, Julian and Cressida

Virginia Nicholson

Writing as sister to two of these artists and daughter to the other, I am the last person to attempt a balanced appraisal of their work. Our lives have intersected too closely for me to be able to stand back, but perhaps I can be illuminating in attempting to speak on their behalf. These two generations have something important in common. Both grew up in the conviction that Art was something everyone could do; that belief was deeply instilled by their – I should say our – upbringing. It wasn't something Other people did, we could do it. Quentin grew up taking it for granted that one's elders and betters painted, and so did his children. In 1963 we welcomed Quentin's return from a lengthy trip abroad with a celebratory exhibition in our playroom, which I expect delighted him. When we went on summer holidays to Charleston, we extended to painting clay pots and statues. We experimented with 'tachisme' too; Quentin showed us how you loaded a paintbrush with very liquid watercolour and spray-spattered it at the paper, and everything else besides. I remember for my tenth birthday Quentin gave me a beautiful box of gouaches, accompanied by a card bearing the lines:

> *With this little box you can*
> *Become, at last, a new Cézanne!*

Unfortunately, inhibitions must have set in at some point in my teens. Not so with Cressida and Julian. Rather to my surprise, both my siblings began to take it all very seriously. Julian launched into a characteristically carefully planned decorative scheme for his bedroom, consisting of enormous psychedelic swirls. At fifteen he was to be found doing meticulous still lifes in tones of white, as an exercise set up for him by Quentin. Cressida had been attracted by bright colours and glittering forms since earliest childhood. When she could barely talk she had a part in a family play where the one line she could be guaranteed to utter confidently was 'Lots and lots of diamonds'. From five she began to collect jewels. As soon as she could she began to learn screenprinting. It must have dawned on Quentin that two out of his three children really meant it about becoming Artists.

Now despite Quentin's innate enthusiasm for the arts, I believe he felt himself to be, at that time, a happy amateur; moreover he was one who had a family to support. Knowing how hard the life of an artist could be, he gently adopted a discouraging posture: he recommended Julian to pursue an academic degree. This only delayed Julian's natural reversion to the artist's path by three years. Cressida was not to be easily dissuaded and she has steadfastly continued to do what she always wanted to do. As for Quentin himself, it is twenty years since he ceased to be an academic. That part of his life can now be seen to have occupied barely more than a quarter of his eighty-five years: the rest has been largely spent in active creation. It's in the genes.

Duncan Grant
Vanessa and Quentin
(*c*.1919)

90

Duncan Grant
Blue Nude (*c*.1928)

Clive Bell

S.P. Rosenbaum

Clive Bell is usually under-estimated by critics and biographers of Bloomsbury. He has always suffered in comparison with Roger Fry, whose greater originality is evidenced by the ideas that Bell begged, borrowed and sometimes (to Fry's irritation) stole from him. Bell was not a painter and claimed not to analyse pictures so much as appreciate them. Bell may, indeed, be the least-liked person in Bloomsbury. He has been found wanting as a husband, as a father, and particularly as a brother-in-law.

It is undeniable that Clive Bell was a wealthy snob, hedonist and womaniser. He cheerfully described himself as 'an honest sensualist', and admitted that his sexuality was 'abnormally normal' (though he was never homophobic). Politically, Bell began as a liberal socialist, became a pacifist during the First World War and an appeaser before the second one. He ended as a reactionary with racist, even anti-Semitic attitudes.

Yet those who knew Clive Bell best in his prime recognised his generosity, charm, tolerance and vitality. His capacity for admiration and enjoyment was second to none in Bloomsbury. Desmond MacCarthy – a great appreciator himself – maintained that it was impossible to over-estimate Clive Bell's role in the making of Bloomsbury, and that Bell's appreciation of his friends' gifts contributed meaningfully to the coherence of the Bloomsbury Group.

Clive Bell's achievements as a writer have also been underrated by Bloomsbury commentators. Two of his books were among the most influential works of his time. The bald titles of *Art* (1914) and *Civilization* (1928) suggest their humorous polemical intent. *Art* had a wider impact than anything Roger Fry wrote. As a modernist tract for Post-Impressionism, it changed both the interpretation of visual art in England and the way that art was written

Duncan Grant
David Garnett (*c*.1916)
In 1916, as Quentin Bell has noted, his mother with 'Duncan Grant, David Garnett, servants, children and a dog arrived at Charleston Farmhouse in order to comply with and perhaps evade the conscription laws of that year'.

about. The book's hypotheses of 'significant form' and 'aesthetic emotion' replace beauty as a subject of aesthetics, and made those phrases current in criticism.

Art has been attacked for circularity, but Bell's theory can easily be reformulated to avoid this. The basic claim is that the aesthetic emotion we feel with certain works of visual art is the result of significant form, which can be described as the relations of forms and combinations of lines and colours in art. More difficult is the essentialism of *Art* (shared with Fry) which leads Bell to argue that all art has a common and peculiar quality, namely significant form. But what has dated *Art* more than anything else is Bell's insistence on the irrelevance of representation in painting and sculpture. This, however, was also part of the ironic exaggeration that *Art* uses to shock conventional purveyors and surveyors of art into paying attention to form instead of content. It was not a view the eclectic Clive Bell held for very long. After the battle for Post-Impressionism was won, he agreed that, though form was still of the essence in art, many other valuable qualities had to be considered as well.

Civilization was written in the aftermath of what was called the war for civilisation. Like *Art* it is based on the premise that the contemplative side of human nature is more valuable than the self-expressive. *Civilization* inquires into what civilisations are not (material prosperity), what the great ones of the past have been (classical Athens, renaissance Italy, eighteenth-century France), and what is now needed for a good one (a rational sense of values). In trying to make people think about what really matters in a civilisation, Bell provokes his readers with the admission that slavery is required – slaves being described as those who 'give some of their surplus time and energy to the support of others'. (Unpaid workers such as house-wives are one of Bell's equivocal examples.) Again there are essentialist flaws in Bell's conception of civilisation, as there are in his notions of art and even of Bloomsbury itself.

Civilization is elaborately dedicated to Virginia Woolf. This did not keep her husband from pointing out in his review that Bell had overlooked the barbarities that were accommodated in his supreme civilisations. The dedicatee herself observed that *Civilization* was good fun, like one of Clive's Bloomsbury luncheon parties. Still, the book had its relevance for Virginia. The next year she would convey a not dissimilar impression of civilisation in the memorable Cambridge luncheon of *A Room of One's Own*. Clive Bell remained for her, as she acknowledged in *Orlando*, the 'most inspiriting of critics'. For readers today he can still be so, if they can find his now shamefully out-of-print books.

Duncan Grant
Decanter and Fruit Dish
(*c*.1916 – 17)
The two principal objects in this watercolour were both at Charleston and appear in several still lifes from 1916 onwards. The fruit dish is seen again in Grant's *Vanessa Bell Painting at Charleston* (see page 40).

Behind the Canvas

Henrietta Garnett

Duncan Grant
The Granary, Charleston
(*c*.1921)

Both my grandparents, Vanessa Bell and Duncan Grant, painted me, it would seem, almost from the time I was born and later at fairly regular intervals until their deaths. My mother-in-law, Frances Partridge, has a charming sketch of me as a baby with a skull as round as Caligula's, hanging on her sitting-room wall. It is by Vanessa. I have in my possession a magnificent Alphabet with full-page illustrations for each letter which Nessa and Duncan made for my elder sister Amaryllis as a Christmas present for her in 1945. She was just over two years old; I was a few months. A is for Amaryllis and shows a portrait of a wide-eyed and somewhat determined looking child – clearly Amaryllis – painted by Nessa. H is for Henrietta with a caution not to wake her. On the opposite page is a painting of a round, chubby baby dressed in a blue frock. She is lying fast asleep in a wicker cradle, one fist in the air. The painting is by Duncan.

Most children accept the environs and conditions into which they are born as the norm. I was no exception. As a child, I took it for granted that the mornings at Charleston would be spent sitting for Nessa and Duncan. The studio itself seemed to me to be a magical place and, as I grew up, I became increasingly aware that it was indeed a sanctum of beauty and unadulterated happiness.

When I was a child, Nessa and Duncan encouraged me to keep still by telling me stories of the past, but as I grew older, they were free to concentrate more intently on their painting. They were generally silent as they painted but they often turned on the wireless and then the splendid large room was filled with the music of Mozart, Beethoven or Bach. Otherwise, the only sounds were the buzz of a fly, the noise of someone knocking a hoe against flint coming from the garden, or the scrape of a knife on the palette. When they did speak, it was sporadi-

OPPOSITE
Duncan Grant
*Girl Painting in the Studio,
Charleston* (*c*.1958)

cally, rather as they squeezed blobs of paint on to the edges of their palettes from time to time. Their remarks might appear to be unconnected, but it was a measure of their intimacy that they needed no explanatory preface. I remember once Duncan professed a deep admiration for the works of Alma-Tadema. Nessa could not resist mocking him in tones of amused affection. Occasionally, we might make some observation about a character in a novel we had been discussing. Or there might be sudden groans from the painters; the light at Charleston is curiously changeable. Naturally, its vagaries affected the painters' perception of colour. With any luck, the cloud would blow away.

Practically everybody I knew painted, or, if they did not actually do so themselves, they were involved to some degree in other people's paintings. My sisters and I drew and painted each other as a matter of course. 'Don't MOVE!' was the constant cry, 'I'm drawing you!' And this demand, it went without saying, overruled whatever it was that one was doing – reading a book, playing the piano or possibly trying to draw someone else.

Nessa generally sat down to paint. She held a fan of brushes in her left hand, the brush she had selected to use in her right, holding it tentatively, like a wand, by the very end of its handle. Then she would make a careful, very deliberate stab at her canvas. She was nothing if not single minded. Her own studio was right at the top of the house. It was a room of very modest proportion but with splendid views of the walled garden, a row of elms and the Weald beyond. It was here that she kept her more personal possessions: a portrait she had painted of her son Julian as a baby; some treasured books in an old packing case which she had decorated and which served as a bookcase; bound volumes of *The Hyde Park Gate News*, the family newspaper she and her brothers and sister had written as children and which she had edited and copied out in her clear, round hand, each page ruled into two columns. I often sat for her in this small and very private space. Perhaps because we were almost always alone up there in her attic studio, she would ask me about my opinions and my hopes for the future. Her advice was always tempered with humour and a sense of the absurd. I enjoyed those sessions greatly and grew to appreciate my grandmother very much. She died when I was just short of sixteen.

After her death, I continued to visit Charleston frequently. It was, indeed, my second home. As time went on, Richard Shone or Simon Watney were frequently there and their youth and enthusiasm helped to invigorate the atmosphere and breathe new life into Duncan as he inspired them. We all had tremendous fun in the studio and yet were perfectly serious at the same time. Later, Richard instigated several painting sessions in London. At one I sat for him and Duncan at Teddy Wolfe's studio in the East End. Another was with Lindy Dufferin at Duncan's pied-à-terre in Patrick Trevor-Roper's house in Regent's Park. They were delightful occasions, the painters' very evident seriousness quite often punctuated by hoots of laughter, and remain fixed in my memory as some of the most enjoyable and educative episodes in my life. Duncan's non sequiturs were unforgettable. But whatever the circumstances, Duncan and Vanessa remained the most dedicated of painters, and the legacy of that is the very great pleasure their pictures bring to so many people who, unlike myself, never had the good fortune to encounter the artists directly, let alone be painted by them.

OPPOSITE
Duncan Grant
Self Portrait (*c*.1909 – 10)

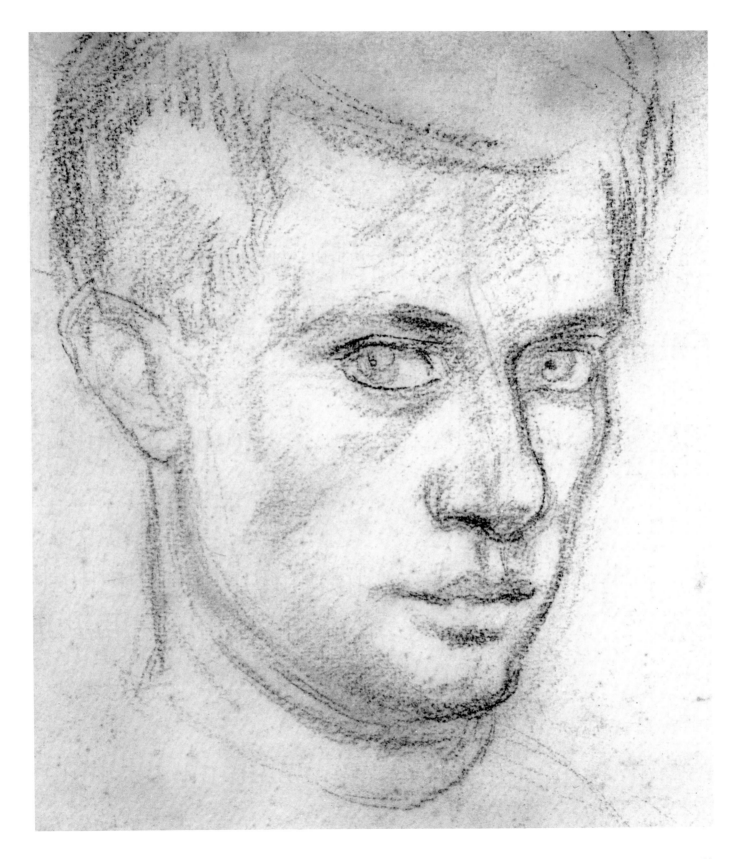

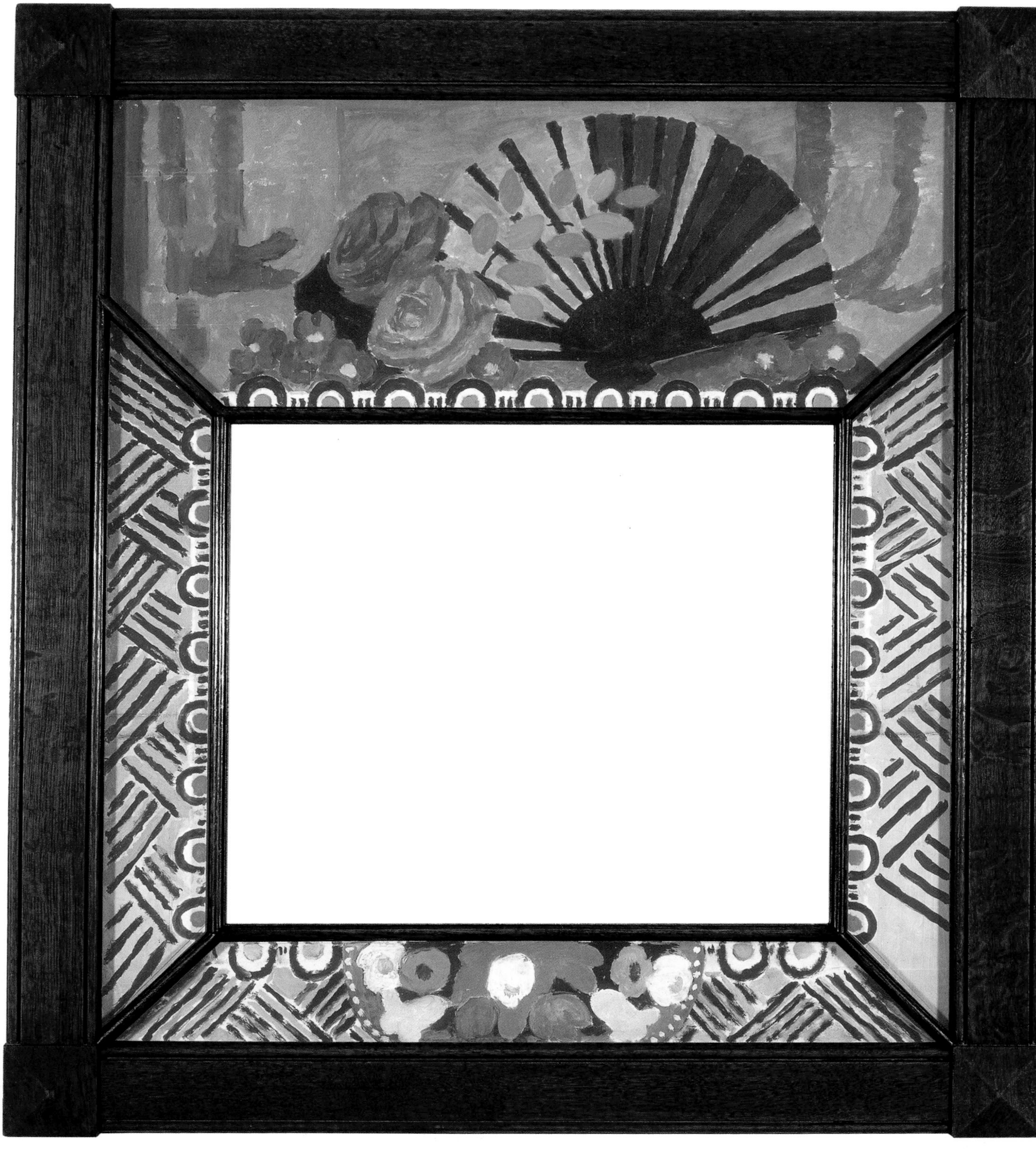

Bloomsbury: Design and Decoration

James Beechey

Vanessa Bell
Table Top Design (1930s)

Towards the end of 1912, energised by the spirited response of a handful of artists to his Post-Impressionist exhibitions, Roger Fry began to formulate an idea for a co-operative studio where the same artists could adapt their talents to applied art, both as a means to earning a living and as an advantage to their work as painters and sculptors. The proposal – which came to fruit the following year as the Omega Workshops – was the logical extension of his crusade for Post-Impressionism, as Fry explained in a begging letter sent to potential backers. 'The Post-Impressionist movement,' he declared, 'is quite as definitely *decorative* in its methods as was the Pre-Raphaelite, and its influence on general *design* is destined to be as marked.'

The vulgarisation of design in Edwardian England appalled Fry. The average man, he complained, regarded a large amount of futile display as a necessary symbol of social status; and he lamented that it was impossible to get a penny or a stamp, let alone a public monument, decently designed. The decorative impulse in English art had long been treated contemptuously by critics for whom decoration was a dirty word, synonymous with frivolity. Even now a tinge of disapproval clings to it. At the Omega, however, Fry and his associates turned the polite notion of good taste on its head. They revelled in spontaneity, cornucopian imagery and, for a time, a riot of brilliant colour. They gave not a jot for decorum, employing a whole menagerie of exotic animals as part of their very individual iconography. A sense of fun pervaded the Workshops: Fry went so far as to describe one Omega chair as 'conversational' and 'witty', the sort he could imagine Max Beerbohm reclining in. The evident pleasure in the making of such a chair was an essential feature of the Omega's approach; and it is the demotic strain which runs through Bloomsbury's attitude to the applied arts that links, despite their stylistic differences, Duncan Grant to Dora Carrington, Roger Fry to Quentin Bell.

OPPOSITE
Vanessa Bell
Mirror Design (1930s)
Design for an embroidered frame for a mirror.

The closure of the Omega in 1919 was hardly a setback to its two leading artists, and 'the firm of Bell and Grant' (as Virginia Woolf christened them) continued to be in demand through the 1920s and 1930s. Most of their commissions came from friends, and many a flat on the Bedford Estate was given the characteristic Bloomsbury make-over. As Richard Shone has written: 'Room after room along the east side of Gordon Square was transformed by nudes and musicians, Mediterranean landscapes and theatrical curtains, fans, flowers, a fountain of arum lilies. There were acres of marbling and stippling bordered by miles of hoops, circles, commas and criss-crosses.' Bell's and Grant's London interiors are known now only from photographs, but elsewhere – in Cambridge, at Rodmell and even in France at Offranville – enough of their decorations survive to suggest something of their gaiety and variety. And, of course, during these years the gradual embellishment of Charleston was in hand, an air of genial and haphazard improvisation belying its surprisingly homogeneous nature.

By the 1930s the insistent linearity that had characterised some of the Omega's most successful products (notably its textiles) had given way in Bell's and Grant's work to a more luxuriant romanticism. Grant's inspired variations on the legends of classical mythology, especially, stood in complete contrast to the prevailing fashion for strict abstractionism, intended to complement austere forms of modern architecture. None the less, they still found favour with private patrons, such as Lady Dorothy Wellesley – whose dining-room at Penns-in-the-Rocks they transformed into a baroque fantasia – and Kenneth Clark – for whom they produced a vast dinner service adorned with portraits of famous women. They also participated in a wide-ranging campaign to involve artists in industry. They drew posters for Shell and dust-jackets for the Hogarth Press; they decorated blanks to be mass-produced by Foley China and Clarice Cliff. Royal Wilton wove carpets to their designs and Allan Walton printed and marketed their textiles. The sorry saga of Cunard's rejection of the panels they had commissioned from Grant for their transatlantic liner the *Queen Mary* was, in fact, the only blot on an otherwise prolific decade.

The most complete advertisement of Bell's and Grant's own exuberant style was the Music Room they installed at the Lefevre Gallery in 1932. It was a show piece for their versatility as designers. They painted six large floral wall panels as well as a gramophone, piano, screen, lamps and vases; curtains and a pelmet were made from Grant's 'Grapes' fabric, and a sofa and chairs were covered in the same material; and the furnishing was completed by two Wilton carpets and an embroidered duet stool. Though this was their last domestic interior, they continued to receive invitations to assist in public projects which, however unexpected, were enthusiastically welcomed. The Charlestonians' well-known disdain for religion was no bar to their collaborating on the decoration of Berwick Church nor to Grant's painting murals for the Russell Chantry at Lincoln Cathedral. During the war they also produced a series of decorations on the theme of Cinderella for Devonshire Hill School in Tottenham; and after it they made wall panels and painted tiles for the graduate hostel at King's College, Cambridge. Grant's long love affair with the theatre found its final expression in his scenery and costumes for John Blow's opera-masque *Venus and Adonis*, first performed at the 1956 Aldeburgh Festival. Designs for a number of these schemes are included in the current exhibition – a reminder that, while the Tate has rightly celebrated their achievements as easel painters, the Bloomsbury artists refused to accept the edges of a canvas as the natural bounds of their abundant creativity.

Vanessa Bell
Alfriston (1931)
A study for a Shell advertisement, the poster itself
was executed in pointillist
style, a rarity for Bell.

OPPOSITE
Duncan Grant
Caryatid (1912 – 13)
This is one of two large
caryatid figures, both using
fabric collage, painted by
Grant in late 1912 or early
1913.

Duncan Grant
*Study for Backdrop for
'Venus and Adonis'* (1956)
A preliminary design for the
opera performed at the
Aldeburgh Festival in 1956.
Grant's designs for the pro-
duction were made at the
invitation of Benjamin
Britten.

Notes on Contributors

James Beechey is a freelance writer whose elegant prose style has found outlet in articles and reviews for the *Charleston Magazine*, the *Financial Times* and the *Burlington Magazine*. He contributed an essay to the catalogue for the Tate Gallery's 'The Art of Bloomsbury' exhibition, and is currently writing a biography of Clive Bell.

Anne Olivier Bell assisted her husband Quentin Bell with his work towards his biography of Virginia Woolf and then herself went on to edit the first complete edition of Virginia Woolf's diary. This five-volume publication provided significant impetus to Woolf studies and brought Olivier Bell an Honorary Degree from the University of York. She continues to live in Sussex where for more than twenty years she has made a major contribution to the affairs of the Charleston Trust.

Julian Bell is the eldest child of Quentin and Anne Olivier Bell. Though first and foremost a painter, he has emerged in recent years as a penetrating art critic in the pages of the *Times Literary Supplement*, the *London Review of Books* and elsewhere. An insight into his perceptive thinking can be gained from his book *What is Painting?* which was highly acclaimed when it appeared in 2000.

Quentin Bell was the second son of Clive and Vanessa Bell, and very widely mourned when he died in 1996. He enjoyed a distinguished academic career at the Universities of Newcastle, Leeds and Sussex, and wrote not only his landmark two-volume biography of Virginia Woolf but also several other books on a number of wide-ranging subjects. In retirement he devoted his time to his delightful, often eccentric, pottery and the affairs of the Charleston Trust.

Tony Bradshaw is the owner of The Bloomsbury Workshop in London which, through its exhibitions over the years, has explored many aspects of Bloomsbury art. He is also the author of the pioneering book, *The Bloomsbury Artists: Prints and Book Design*, a comprehensive catalogue of the work done in this field.

Angelica Garnett is the daughter of Vanessa Bell and Duncan Grant. Her own creativity has found an outlet through mosaics, painting, sculpture and writing, and her memoir *Deceived With Kindness* has made a unique contribution to Bloomsbury studies.

Henrietta Garnett is the second daughter of David and Angelica Garnett. She made her debut as a writer with her novel *Family Skeletons*, and is currently at work on a book about Anne Thackeray Ritchie. Like her mother, she has chosen to live and work in France.

Craufurd Goodwin is Duke Professor of Economics at Duke University in the United States. His ability to combine an interest in Bloomsbury with economics resulted in his book *Art and the Market: Roger Fry on Commerce in Art*, and more recently he has expanded on this interest in *Economic Engagements with Art*. With his wife Nancy, he possesses an outstanding collection of Bloomsbury art, held at their beautiful home in North Carolina.

Jane Hill is the author of *The Art of Dora Carrington*. Subsequently she was the curator of the highly successful Dora Carrington exhibition at the Barbican Art Gallery in 1995.

Hermione Lee is an outstanding academic, critic and broadcaster. Her publications include two biographies, of Willa Cather and Virginia Woolf, the latter receiving international acclaim. She has taught at the Universities of Liverpool and York and is currently the Goldsmiths' Professor of English at Oxford University.

Virginia Nicholson is the elder daughter of Quentin and Anne Olivier Bell. She helped complete the attractively illustrated and well-documented book on Charleston which was begun by her father, is actively involved with the Charleston Trust and is currently working on a new book. She is married to the playwright and scriptwriter Bill Nicholson and lives in Sussex.

Nigel Nicolson, the younger son of Harold Nicolson and Vita Sackville-West, has had a distinguished and varied career as soldier, politician, publisher and author. His many books include his well-received autobiography, his revelatory account of his parents' unorthodox marriage, a biography of Napoleon, and the six volumes of Virginia Woolf's letters which he edited with Joanne Trautmann. He continues to live at the family home, Sissinghurst.

Frances Partridge, 101 at the date of publication, is the only person living, apart from Angelica Garnett, to have known all the central characters within the Bloomsbury Group. After leaving Cambridge University she worked at the Birrell and Garnett bookshop and her subsequent friendship with Clive Bell and marriage to Ralph Partridge, after the death of his first wife Dora Carrington, drew her into the heart of Bloomsbury. Her published diaries, starting with *A Pacifist's War*, rank her among the important British diarists of the twentieth century.

S.P. Rosenbaum is the leading literary historian of Bloomsbury, with many publications to his name, notably *The Bloomsbury Group* and, more recently, *Aspects of Bloomsbury*. Now retired from his professorship at the University of Toronto, he lives near Halifax, Nova Scotia.

Richard Shone is Bloomsbury's leading art historian. His book *Bloomsbury Portraits* (1976) was the first serious analysis of the work of Duncan Grant and Vanessa Bell and this ultimately led to his appointment in 1999/2000 as curator of the Tate Gallery's 'The Art of Bloomsbury' exhibition which later travelled to two venues in the USA. Shone's catalogue for this exhibition is a defining record of Bloomsbury art.

Frances Spalding is an art historian, critic and biographer and has written the lives of three Bloomsbury figures – Roger Fry, Vanessa Bell and Duncan Grant. Her centenary history of the Tate Gallery was the first full account of this national institution, and her *British Art since 1900* remains a useful, lively and informative introduction to the art of this period. Her biography *Gwen Raverat: Friends, Family and Affections* has recently been published.

Editor's Acknowledgements

I am most grateful to the copyright holders of the estates of Vanessa Bell, Dora Carrington, Roger Fry and Duncan Grant for permission to reproduce the work of these artists.

With the exception of Nigel Nicolson's piece, copyright for all the essay texts rests with The Bloomsbury Workshop but I am appreciative of the authors' willing co-operation in the republishing of their essays in book form. An extract from *The Letters of Virginia Woolf* published by the Hogarth Press is reprinted by permission of The Random House Group Ltd and Harcourt Brace Inc.

A number of people have assisted greatly in allowing their pictures to be photographed for this publication. These include Jeremy Hill, Craufurd and Nancy Goodwin, Douglas Liebhafsky and Wendy Gimbel, Ray Roberts, David and Cassandra Harris, Patricia Barnes, Andrew King, Sybil del Strother, Robert Reedman, Susan Chaires, Roger Eastman, Paul Sardelli, Allen and Anne Dick, Angela Buchanan, Pierre and Marie-Madelaine Coumans, Patrizia Bellman, Jane Pritchard, Roger and Hazel Silver as well as a number of other private collectors.

Others who have contributed in various ways include Richard Shone, Regina Marler, Frances Spalding, Sue Fox, Eleanor Moreton and Kate Kennedy. Their assistance has been invaluable.

Finally, I record my appreciation of the considerable contribution made by my son, Mark Bradshaw, who not only took the photographs but also designed the book. His skill and his creativity significantly enhance *A Bloomsbury Canvas*.

List of Illustrations

Vanessa Bell (1879 – 1961)

In addition to the works by the Bloomsbury artists detailed above, there is a painting of *Clive Bell* by the Duchesse de La Rochefoucauld shown on page 93.